The Long-Awaited Sequel to 'N

MARKETPLACE AMBASSADORS

CBMC's Continuing Legacy of Evangelism and Disciplemaking

Robert J. Tamasy

© 2019, Christian Business Men's Connection
All rights reserved
Chattanooga, Tennessee 37414
www.cbmc.com

Printed in the United States of America
ISBN 978-1-947457-18-8 First paperback printing.

Cover design: Scott Rasmussen/Ras Graphics, Inc.

*Dedicated to the past CBMCers
who built the foundation and left a legacy,
to current CBMCers who are building on
that foundation, and to future CBMCers
who will embrace the vision and continue
the legacy of fulfilling the Great Commission to
men in the marketplace – to the glory
of the Lord Jesus Christ.*

Table of Contents

Foreword
Introduction

1. Losing It All – and Gaining Much More 1
2. CBMC, the Early Days 11
3. Moving From Death to Life 23
4. A New Face for the Ministry 35
5. 'Satisfied Customers' 49
6. The Importance of Follow-Through....................................59
7. Evangelism: A Process, Not an Event..................................67
8. Advancing Into the Urban Marketplace...............................73
9. Like Father, Like Son..79
10. Marketplace Ambassadors 85
11. A Tale of Two (Very Different) Cities 93
12. Enough Ministry For a Lifetime.......................................107
13. Transitions in Leadership..115
14. CBMC Enters the Digital World..121
15. Communicating the Mission of the Movement 127
16. Going Into All the World 133
17. Women and Families – Not Forgotten By CBMC....................141
18. To the Next Generation – and Beyond 149

Appendix 1: Calling and Mission
Appendix 2: What CBMC Is and Is Not

Foreword

This book has been a long time in coming. Years ago I read a little book called *Men Aflame*, written by David R. Enlow, which recounted the founding and early days of CBMC. I still find myself referring to it often to this day, but it ends around 1970, recapping only the first 40 years of CBMC.

CBMC has now been actively and faithfully serving the Lord Jesus Christ in the marketplace for nearly 90 years, and as you can imagine, a lot has happened in and through the ministry since 1970. So I'm very excited that this new volume, *Marketplace Ambassadors,* has finally been published to bring the amazing and inspiring story of this ministry up to date. As you'll learn by reading this book, CBMC has a rich heritage and legacy which continues to grow by the day.

My own history with CBMC dates back to 1971, even though I didn't realize that until almost two decades later. When I was 18, I attended a Youth for Christ summer camp at the LeTourneau Christian Campgrounds on Canandaigua Lake, in Canandaigua, New York. I came to know Jesus Christ as my Savior at that camp, but it wasn't until 1989, after moving to Fredericksburg, Virginia with my family to take a new job, that I discovered that R.G. LeTourneau, who had built the campground in upstate New York, was one of CBMC's founding fathers in the 1930s.

I may be one of the rare individuals who attended his first CBMC event without being invited. I saw an announcement posted at a church about a CBMC banquet, and decided to check it out. There were about 150 people in attendance. I saw businessmen sharing life stories – their testimonies – and talking about the Bible, telling how it related to their lives. At the close, one of them prayed and invited the guests to fill out cards and indicate if they wanted to learn more about what they had heard. I had never been exposed to anything like this, and it grabbed a hold of my heart.

For years I had been searching for something like that. I had even tried to do it on my own as a businessman in Connecticut before relocating to Fredericksburg. It amazed me to see men with a vision and strategy for reaching out to others in the name of Christ.

Not long afterward, someone gave me a copy of *Men Aflame*. I became captivated by the story of CBMC's beginnings, as well as the passion and dedication of the men who saw how their roles as business and professional men and followers of Jesus Christ could – and should – work together. It told some of the stories of men upon whose humble yet determined shoulders we in CBMC stand today. One of them mentioned in the book was R.G. LeTourneau, one of CBMC's early leaders, and that's how I discovered the connection with the LeTourneau campground.

Years later, after becoming Chairman of the CBMC Board of Directors, I had the opportunity to meet Roy LeTourneau, R.G.'s son. I had the privilege of spending time with Roy, talking about his father and learning about Roy's own experiences with CBMC.

This book recaptures some of what I've read in *Men Aflame,* but primarily unfolds what God has been doing through CBMC since that time, how the ministry has sharpened and refined its focus to evangelizing and discipling business and professional men. It tells how we've come to this point, and where we believe the Lord is taking CBMC as we anticipate celebrating its 100th anniversary not too many years from now.

I hope you'll be just as excited about reading *Marketplace Ambassadors* as I was when I consumed the earlier book. If you're already involved in CBMC, this will provide you with a better understanding of the people, events and developments that helped bring us to where we are today. If you're new to CBMC, or simply wanting to learn more about it, this book is for you as well.

Most of all, my prayer is that God will use it to mobilize you in your own ministry where you work, as well as where you live. Jesus told us to "let your light shine before men, that they may see your good deeds and praise your Father in heaven" (Matthew 5:16). We find ourselves in times when the darkness sometimes seems overwhelming. But we know it's no match for the light of Christ, shining through His people. Especially in the marketplace.

> – *Bill McAvinney*
> *President, CBMC*
> *2019*

Introduction

"Legacy." We hear and use this term a lot these days. Perhaps it's because the huge Baby Boomer generation is aging and many of its members, increasingly aware that their most productive years are fading, have shifted their life's focus from success to significance. They're wondering how large of a ripple they've made in this pond we call everyday life.

This isn't a bad thing. Although we must live one day at a time, there's also a desire to know we've made an impact, that this world is somehow different – hopefully better – for our having been here. What will our own legacy be?

It's for this reason that *Marketplace Ambassadors* has been written: To recount and celebrate the rich and growing legacy of the ministry called CBMC, and acknowledge some of the devoted and visionary people who helped build it into a movement God has used for nearly 90 years to touch and transform the hearts and lives of countless thousands – perhaps even millions – of men, their wives, families, companies and communities.

You're probably familiar with the saying, "Those who forget history are doomed to repeat it." There's a corollary to that truth, that those who forget history often fail to learn about and appreciate the solid framework that was established by those who preceded them. In revisiting the history of CBMC, our desire isn't to create pedestals for the ministry or the faithful people who were involved in leading it, but to recognize their roles in helping to lay the strong foundation upon which CBMC now stands.

So, in that respect, we can say – without magnifying those who have gone before – that CBMC today stands on the shoulders of giants, men of deep faith and conviction, whose overwhelming mission and motivation were to serve the Lord in the marketplace and be His ambassadors where they worked and wherever their professions took them.

My personal experience with CBMC began in 1981, when I applied for the staff editor position at the Chattanooga-based national office. Prior to learning about the job opening, I'd never heard of CBMC. There had been no vital CBMCs in either Columbus, Ohio or Houston, Texas, where I had worked as a newspaper editor. After being interviewed at CBMC's national office and touring the facility, however, I knew I would enjoy working with the ministry.

There was one problem: I was still a relatively new believer, only a few years into my walk with Jesus, still rather damp behind the ears spiritually. Suspecting a "spiritual giant" would be selected to fill the role, I flew home feeling utterly unqualified.

God had different ideas, however. In His providence, about two weeks later I received a phone call at my office in Tomball, Texas, outside of Houston, where I served as the editor of a community newspaper. Duane Jacobs, then CBMC's Director of Administration, was calling to offer me the job. I eagerly accepted, a moment that would mark the beginning of a professional and spiritual adventure that in many ways has continued to this day.

One of the joys of writing this book is the opportunity to introduce you, the reader, to some folks you may never have heard of, or whose names might sound somewhat familiar even though you know little about them. Since 1981, God has enabled me to cross paths with thousands of outstanding, Christ-centered individuals, some of whom have served as role models and mentors for me. You will find a number of them among the individuals discussed in this book.

My trepidation is being unable to mention everyone who deserves some sort of recognition. But my hope is that by telling stories about some of these faithful followers of Jesus, they will serve as representative of the contributions by thousands of others whose stories and testimonies could also have been told.

Today, CBMC is a growing, vibrant marketplace ministry engaged in changing the world in the name of Jesus Christ one life, one family, one business at a time. What it looks like today is very different from what it looked like soon after its founding in 1930 (as you will discover in the second chapter), or even when I first became a "CBMCer" back in the early 1980s.

What hasn't changed is its vision, purpose and godly calling. CBMC continues to pursue its longtime "twofold mission," that being "to present Jesus Christ as Savior and Lord to business and professional men, and to develop Christian business and professional men to carry out the Great Commission."

Along with Jesus' command to "make disciples of all nations" (Matthew 28:19), CBMC has maintained a sharp, steady focus on the multi-generational vision of 2 Timothy 2:2, "The things which you have heard from me in the presence of many witnesses, entrust these to faithful men who will be able to teach others also."

My hope is that by the time you finish reading this book, you'll not only have a greater understanding of the history of CBMC and the legacy of those who have gone before, but also will be more excited and committed to this unique work: Taking the Good News of Jesus Christ to the people in the marketplace of the 21st century – small entrepreneurial ventures, medium-sized businesses, large corporations, and everywhere in between – and helping to equip those who come to know Him to grow spiritually and learn how to reach out to others in His name.

– *Robert J. Tamasy*
2019

Chapter 1 –

Losing It All – and Gaining Much More

*"For what does it profit a man to gain the whole world,
and forfeit his soul?" – Mark 8:36*

You could consider it an epic plunge, a dramatic descent from penthouse to doghouse. For months his name appeared in front page articles in major national publications, but not for good reasons.

Mark Whitacre had been experiencing the life most business executives could only imagine. He had attained a seven-figure income, had a beautiful wife, three wonderful children attending the best private schools, a mansion, cars, stellar academic credentials, and a career certain to position him as chief executive of a huge food additive company ranked 56th largest on the Fortune 500 at the time. Everything the so-called American dream could possibly promise.

At 32, Mark had become the youngest divisional president in the company's history, and three years later was promoted to corporate vice president and corporate officer. He was the likely choice to become COO and president as soon as the 70-year-old president retired.

Then it all came crashing down.

Outward appearances of success and luxury had concealed an inner misery only his wife, Ginger, perceived. "People would drive by our home and say, 'Mark Whitacre has it all!' What they did not know is that I had a void in my heart the size of the Grand Canyon," he admitted.

What his wife could see that others could not was her husband in deep conflict, torn by reaping great material rewards from participating in what later was termed the largest price-fixing scandal in U.S. history.

"In 1992, Ginger noticed big changes in me. Work consumed me. She could sense I was not happy," Mark said. "I was greedy. No matter how much I earned, it was never enough."

He attended church with his family, "but I was just going through the motions." It was Ginger who possessed spiritual strength, a faith in Jesus Christ she's drawn from since she was 13 years old. It was that faith, along with her unwavering convictions about doing what's right, that led Mark to abandon the career MBAs fantasize about to face the grim realities of what he and his industry peers were doing.

"It was November 5, 1992. I remember the day very well. Ginger started digging deeper into our conversations, asking direct questions like: What was going on at work? Why was I so intense? Why did I seem so unhappy? Finally, I told her the very top executives at our company – including myself – were engaged in illegal activity, getting together with our competitors and fixing prices on several key ingredients.

"We had formed what amounted to an international cartel, stealing a billion dollars each year from our large food and beverage customers. That increased cost was being passed on to consumers, so we basically were stealing from everyone around the world who bought groceries."

Appalled at what she heard, Ginger insisted that Mark turn himself in to the FBI. He responded that he could go to prison, and it would cost them their home, cars and lavish lifestyle. But she retorted she would rather be homeless than live in a home paid for by theft. "'Either turn yourself in to the FBI, or I will do it for you,' she told me, and I knew she meant it," he recalled.

An hour later, persuaded by a 34-year-old, stay-at-home mom who clung to a faith he did not possess, Mark was confessing to an FBI agent the white-collar crime that he, his company, and several other international companies had been engaging in for years.

Federal authorities were not interested in prosecuting just a single individual who had admitted to participation in a global price-fixing scandal. They wanted to take down the entire operation and everyone involved, especially the kingpins that had been doing price-fixing for a decade before Mark even joined the company. Therefore, they offered Mark a deal – full immunity from prosecution in the case, in exchange for working undercover with the FBI, wearing a wire to covertly record all of his business interactions. This included price-fixing meetings not only at the company's Decatur, Illinois headquarters but also in cities around the world – Paris, Mexico City, Vancouver, Hong Kong, Zurich and others.

The one condition of the immunity agreement was that he could not break any laws the FBI did not already know about.

"Working undercover was an extremely stressful life, a life at odds with itself. I acted like a loyal executive, building the company during the day and tearing it down during the evenings. I would meet with the FBI at 6 a.m., when they would shave my chest to tape mini-microphones, check batteries in the tape recorders in my briefcase, and review a special FBI notebook I had to maintain. I would record my peers during the day, then meet with the FBI again at various hotels from 6 p.m. to midnight to turn over the tapes and endure debriefings that seemed endless.

"After two years of wearing the wire, I was spent mentally and emotionally. I no longer knew whether I worked for the FBI or the food additive company. This left me totally confused, spiraling out of control, feeling like I was on the verge of a nervous breakdown."

The extent of Mark's disorientation became evident when one night at 3 a.m., during a horrific thunderstorm, he took a leaf blower out to the driveway and tried clearing leaves "to keep up appearances. I was even in my shirt and tie." Hearing the commotion, Ginger peered out their bedroom window and then, sheltered by an umbrella, went out to confront her husband.

She yelled to him, "You need to come back into the house. You need to come back to your family. More than anything, you need to have God in your life!" Mark responded, "Who needs God? I am going to be the next president of the 56th largest company in America!"

Her reaction took him off-guard. "She looked as angry as I have ever seen her. At that moment, as she's said on several TV interviews over the years, 'Divorce was never an option – but murder was.' Then she told me, 'I am proud of what you are doing, the fact that you are working with the FBI, but you are not going to be president of the company. You need to get that fact through your mind. You will not be able to stay there after they learn you are the mole. You are bringing the top three executives above you down; they are likely to go to jail. You will be fired once they learn what you've done. You need to realize that fact.'

"She left me in the driveway, and I knew she was right. I would not be able to stay at the company, but could not imagine living without that position and income. I was addicted to success and obsessed with material things, so I began to think about how to protect myself."

Years later Mark was diagnosed as being bipolar, a condition caused by a chemical imbalance in the brain that if untreated not only induces extreme mood shifts but also can bring about major lapses in judgment. This prompted his next ill-advised course of action.

"I determined to steal what would have been my severance pay, $9.5 million. If the company learned of my plot to steal this money and accused me, I would challenge them, saying how could they prosecute me for stealing millions when they were stealing billions? I felt immune, so I decided to submit several bogus invoices from small companies I owned until they had paid me the $9.5 million to which I felt entitled.

"About this scheme I consulted no one, not even Ginger. I felt protected, but was actually isolated and wounded. In retrospect, I realized I should have talked to someone."

That eventually led to the collapse of everything Mark held dear. In June 1995, when his company learned he had been the informant that exposed the elaborate price-fixing conspiracy, executives immediately contacted the FBI and news media. "They notified them I was no white knight, that I had stolen $9.5 million. The gig was up, and I lost the immunity agreement."

Mark Whitacre's name began appearing prominently in national publications, including *USA Today, Wall Street Journal,* and *FORTUNE* magazine, and a subject of much TV coverage, but that was not good news.

Even with this, all was not lost for Mark. Not yet. Even though the FBI agents with whom he had worked nearly three years had ample reason for rejecting him, they still supported him and helped obtain an outstanding attorney to represent him. They worked behind the scenes to aid in getting him a plea deal that would minimize a prison sentence.

This was hardly an act of kindness or compassion. They reasoned Mark was the highest-ranked executive in U.S. history to become a whistle blower. Prosecuting him could discourage others with similar status from one day coming forward. They understood the poor decisions he made had occurred while he was mentally unstable. And lastly, they knew before agents go undercover, they receive years of extensive training and regular mental health counseling to assist them in dealing with the conflict of living a double life. Mark had received absolutely no training or counseling.

Based on this information, prosecutors agreed to a three-year plea deal. However, Mark's attorney felt by presenting the same arguments to the presiding judge, the penalty could be whittled down to a six-month prison sentence.

"The lawyer called Ginger and me to his office in Chicago to review details of what he termed 'the deal of a lifetime.' Then I proved I was still my own worst enemy by rejecting the deal and firing my attorney," Mark said. "Instead, I hired new attorneys and started preparing to go to trial rather than take the plea deal.

"I could have taken my Chicago attorney's counsel with humility. I should have been broken at that point. Decisions I had made in the isolation of my own mind were coming back to haunt me."

Mark's hubris-fueled plan, boldly assuming he could avoid prison time altogether, backfired and in the fall of 1997, he received a 10½-year prison sentence. Soon the ramifications of his foolhardy decision became obvious, Mark admitted. "How would I survive a decade in prison? How would my family survive?"

In the federal prison system, there is no parole; that option had been eliminated in the mid-1980s. Defendants could receive a 15 percent sentence reduction for good behavior, but even that best-case scenario meant Mark would be incarcerated a minimum of eight years, eight months.

His greatest fear concerned his family. "How would they go on without me? *Would* they go on without me?" He had already missed much of his children's lives, initially due to his out-of-balance commitment to work, and then his undercover role with the FBI. He read that 99 percent of those in prison for five years or more become divorced.

"I reasoned there was no way my marriage could survive this ordeal. And how would they support themselves? Ginger had not worked outside the home for more than a decade, and we had lost everything – the house, cars, stock, and our savings. I wondered if I would ever be employed as a convicted felon."

Despair and hopelessness set in for Mark as his dismal future loomed. He had been sentenced in September 1997 and set to report to prison on March 4, 1998. "In the months before entering prison, I was emotionally and spiritually bankrupt. I did not want to live, and doubted that I deserved to live. I knew my life insurance policy would grant a death benefit if I took my own life, and convinced there was no other solution, attempted suicide twice, which landed me in the hospital as I spiraled even deeper into depression."

In part to escape constant scrutiny in the small Illinois community where they had lived, Mark and his family relocated to Chapel Hill, North Carolina. Despite his conviction, he had been hired to serve as CEO of a small biotech company there. This move proved to be providential, beginning a new chapter of redemption and restoration.

His first suicide attempt had come shortly after refusing the plea deal, but he made another attempt after they moved to Chapel Hill, still without hope for his future. A CBMC member, Ian Howes, read about Mark's case and attempts on his own life, and decided to call on him personally.

Ian was also a high-level executive in the biotech industry. They had crossed paths over the years at professional conferences, although Mark did not recall their encounters.

"I'll never forget Ian Howes' first sentence when he came to see me. He said, 'Prison's going to be the beginning of your life, and you're going to find the true purpose for your life through the journey you're ready to begin.' More than 20 years later, I'm amazed at how true that statement proved to be. But at the time, it sounded crazy and was hard to process."

Almost immediately, Mark found a glimmer of hope at a desperate time. "Ian was about the same age as me, and since he was in my sphere of influence, a peer in our industry, I respected him from the beginning. He showed genuine interest in me as a person and listened to my story without condemning. There was something different about him, something I had not seen in other friendships.

"I started thinking, maybe I shouldn't kill myself. Maybe there's a little hope here. It was like being offered a lifeline. It made me want to explore what he had in mind."

What Ian had in mind was to get Mark into the Scriptures, helping him to discover who Jesus Christ is, along with His offer of love, grace and mercy.

"He took me through a booklet called *First Steps,* which addressed questions such as, is the Bible credible, who was Jesus, what did He do, and what difference did it make. Then Ian guided me through the Gospel of John, and then we started in *Operation Timothy.* Each week he planted seeds of the Gospel in me that would ultimately lead me to Christ. He assured me that Jesus had already forgiven me, many in society would forgive me, and that God would keep my family together even while I was in prison."

Before starting his prison sentence, Mark joined Ian at some CBMC meetings and observed him at work, seeing for the first time what a servant leader looks like, "even though I didn't know at the time what that meant.

"Ian cared so much about his employees, vendors, and people in general. I couldn't stop thinking that this guy was really different. I was used to stepping on other people to move up in the industry. Ian became a mentor for me, slowly undoing what other 'mentors' had taught me to do wrong."

When Mark entered federal prison in Springfield, Missouri on March 4, 1998, he became inmate No. 07543424. Soon afterward, he was transferred to the federal penitentiary in Yazoo, Mississippi. Ian remained in touch with him during his entire time of incarceration, talking with him by phone and writing letters. But God brought another man into Mark's life, Charles Colson, who himself had served time in prison as a key figure in the Watergate scandal as one of President Richard Nixon's chief aides, called by some his "hatchet man."

After himself coming to Christ and being discipled while in prison, Colson had founded Prison Fellowship, a ministry dedicated to helping prisoners discover a relationship with the Lord and prepare them for life outside of prison upon their release.

Colson became one of Mark's mentors, sharing the same truths from the Bible that Ian had taught him. "He said that God loved me, and no matter what mistakes I had made, God could forgive me. At first, I thought the damage I had done and mistakes I had made were too huge for God to forgive. But then I read 1 John 1:9, which says, 'But if we confess our sins to him, he is faithful and just to forgive us our sins and to cleanse us from all wickedness.'

"Both Ian and Chuck told me God had sent His only Son, Jesus, to live on earth and die on the cross to pay the penalty for my sins so I might be made right with God – for *all* my sins, not just those I committed at the food additive company. And for the first time, I realized from the Bible that I could go to heaven and have eternal life by putting my faith in what Jesus accomplished on the cross and believing He had been raised from the dead.

"I got it! I finally understood being a Christian is not about going to church every Sunday, or what I did or didn't do. It was about a relationship with God. In June 1998, in a prison cell, I got on my knees, asked God to forgive me, and surrendered to Christ. At last I had peace."

Even though he was only three months into a sentence that could last more than 10 years, Mark felt content. As Ian had predicted, instead of signifying the end of his life, going to prison proved to be the beginning of Mark's life, born again into a new, eternal life in Christ. This was the first, but not the last, of many miracles God would be doing.

After his conversion, and full of zeal for his Savior, Mark began ministering to many of his fellow inmates, taking more than 60 of them through *Operation Timothy*, as Ian had done for him.

God enabled him to "beat the odds" by having his marriage survive, and even thrive, during his nearly nine years of incarceration. Because of Ginger's faith in Christ, her love for Mark and commitment to their marriage never wavered. Mark was relocated three times during his sentence, and each time his family moved to be near the prison. His wife and children faithfully visited him every Friday, Saturday, Sunday and holiday during the entire time.

God provided for his family while he was in prison. Several large companies that won major class action judgments against the food additive corporations volunteered to assist them because Mark had stepped forward. A third miracle was that when Mark was released on December 21, 2006, even being a convicted felon and 49 years old, he was hired by Cypress Systems, Inc., a biotech company, as COO and chief operating officer.

Because the company had an office in Pensacola, Florida, Mark reconnected with CBMC and soon was discipling other men. Then came a totally unexpected opportunity that would alter the course of the rest of his life and career. He was invited to give his testimony at a CBMC outreach meeting in Chapel Hill on May 7, 2009, at the invitation of his good friend and spiritual mentor, Ian.

"I did it out of respect for him, but said I would never do that again. However, another invitation came from Bill Montross, a CBMC leader in Charlotte, North Carolina, and then Harold Armstrong, a staff member in Oklahoma City, asked me to speak at CBMC's annual leadership prayer breakfast there. Since then, God has opened the doors for me to speak at hundreds of CBMC events, including 96 times in 2017 alone."

With his wrongdoings behind him, Mark joined the CBMC staff full-time in July 2013, speaking at outreach events and making presentations at a variety of meetings to cast vision for the Marketplace Ambassador initiative. He later became National Director of Field Operations, and in January 2017 added the title of COO.

"What a joy and privilege it is for me to live what I'm able to share around the country, the transforming power of Jesus Christ in the lives of a man, his family, friends and people with whom he works," Mark said. "God is truly able to do exceeding abundantly beyond anything we could ever ask or imagine."

This testimony of Mark Whitacre's changed life is amazing, even incredible, but it's merely one of countless thousands of similar stories of God transforming lives through the ministry of CBMC. With 2020 marking its 90th year of ministry, the Lord has used CBMC to touch the lives and hearts of people in the business and professional community, not only across the United States, but also around the globe.

To understand how far CBMC has come over those years – and where we believe God will be taking it in future – a brief look at its past will help to more fully appreciate the rich heritage and legacy of the bold, dedicated and visionary men involved in its founding. This is the focus of the next chapter, taking a step back to 1930, a time of great turmoil and despair for the United States and much of the world.

Chapter 2

CBMC, the Early Days

*"…there went with him a band of men, whose hearts
God had touched." – 1 Samuel 10:26*

It's hard for most of us to imagine what it must have been like for people trying to survive during the Great Depression of the 1930s. Today, the Depression exists only as a period of distant history, a fading memory for a shrinking segment of people still living. In 1930, however, life in the United States was marked with unprecedented despair that knew no social boundaries.

As the economic calamities set in, countless men, women and their families spiraled into hopelessness. Jobs were lost, food and everyday essentials became scarce, and financial woes beset nearly everyone to some extent. Where were they to turn?

After fervent prayer, a small band of Christian businessmen in Chicago – and several other cities soon after – stepped up to address the spiritual malaise. These individuals were coping with hardships of their own, but determined to do what they could to present the hope and peace only the Gospel of Jesus Christ could provide for such a dire time. Little did they know that they were laying the foundation for a vibrant ministry called CBMC, which God continues to use many decades later to touch the lives of business and professional men, their families, friends, coworkers, companies and communities.

This was a *Kairos* moment, an ancient Greek word that describes a unique, opportune time when God is doing a great work. Think of Abraham, a humble, faithful man who became "the father of many nations." Or Gideon, whom the Lord commanded to lead 300 men into battle against Midianites and Amalekites "as numerous as locusts." Or Jonah, a reluctant voice God used to spark revival in the pagan city of Nineveh. Or the handful of sometimes puzzled apostles that Jesus left behind to establish His Church.

In a similar way, starting in 1930, small bands of Christian businessmen were seizing their own Kairos opportunity. In response to increasing spiritual

openness among men and women facing desperate circumstances, CBMC
– known for many years as the Christian Business Men's Committee –
emerged.

When committees of Christian business leaders formed, first in Chicago
and then in San Francisco and several other cities, the intent was not to spawn
a nationwide network comprised of thousands of business and professional
men serving as ambassadors for Jesus Christ in today's workplace. They
could not have imagined such a thing. Their vision was simple: To pray for
the United States and seek the Lord's guidance for bringing eternal hope to
people in the grips of economic despair and personal crisis.

Original members of the group in Chicago were A.J. Leaman, C.B.
Hedstrom, J.S. Lincoln, Frank W. Sheriff, and Ernest Wadsworth of the
Great Commission Prayer League. These names may no longer be familiar
for many of us, but their legacy has been a lasting one. They first met
regularly for prayer, seeking God's wisdom and direction. Together they
settled on the name Christian Business Men's Committee, reasoning that
working in concert as a "committee," each member would be responsible
for specific duties.

As years passed, CBMC's mission would become more sharply defined,
focusing on reaching and discipling business and professional men for
Jesus Christ. However, original efforts were broader in scope, envisioning a
citywide spiritual impact.

One of the group's first projects was to sponsor Monday-Friday noon-
hour Gospel services at the Grand Opera House in Chicago's Loop. To
reach all parts of the city, the services were broadcast over radio station
WJJD. Through that strategy, thousands of men and women responded,
praying to commit their lives to Christ.

Radio continued to be CBMC's medium of choice for many years.
Services were later aired over WMBI, the flagship radio station for
Moody Bible Institute, and a program called "Man to Man" – 15-minute,
taped interviews with business and professional men – was produced to
communicate the Gospel and inspire believers.

Broadcasts continued well into the 1950s, prompting CBMC to
eventually adopt the motto, "Broadcasting the Gospel." A lapel pin was
even designed bearing the image of a radio microphone to represent that
mission.

Slowly the vision began to expand for Christians in the business world to collaborate in spreading the Gospel in other cities. In 1936, Dr. Paul W. Rood, president of the Bible Institute of Los Angeles (BIOLA), approached Arnold Grunigen, Jr., general sales manager for a San Francisco investment firm, to tell him what he had learned about the work of CBMC in Chicago.

"CBMC is reaching men I can't reach," Rood told him. "They're invited to lunch, they hear a few testimonies, and are offered proof that Christianity does work."

Under Grunigen's leadership, San Francisco joined Chicago in having a full-fledged CBMC. By 1938, five city-based committees had been formed, prompting a general conference that was held at Chicago's LaSalle Hotel. The meeting attracted about 150 CBMC members who elected a five-person steering committee: Charles E. Gremmels, president of a New York real estate and investment company; Grunigen; Hedstrom, a Swedish immigrant who had become a shoe merchant; N.A. Jepson, a Seattle chiropractor; and R.G. LeTourneau of Longview, Texas, also an industrialist.

Hedstrom became the first chairman of the still-young CBMC movement, and LeTourneau was named vice chairman. Grunigen served as secretary, and Jepson assumed the role of treasurer.

By 1941, CBMC had moved beyond U.S. borders for the first time, with a committee established in London, Ontario, Canada. It joined with other new groups in Philadelphia, Detroit, Los Angeles, Seattle, and San Diego. Incorporated as Christian Business Men's Committee International (CBMCI), members gathering for the fourth annual convention in Philadelphia elected LeTourneau as the first international chairman.

Among those serving on the international board of directors was Robert A. Laidlaw of Auckland, New Zealand, who became the author of *The Reason Why*, a booklet that CBMC members have utilized for many years as an evangelistic tool.

Seeking to continue the expansion of the mission and vision of CBMC, Blair Quick and Charles Cooper in 1943 became the first traveling representatives for CBMC, and others assumed that role in years that followed, including Theodore E. McCully and LeTourneau. CBMC also began a practice of working in partnership with churches and other Christian ministries, always looking for new ideas and methods for reaching others with the Good News of Jesus Christ.

By this time, CBMC had begun diversifying its "toolbox" beyond the realm of radio. Open-air evangelistic meetings, along with events in hospitals, jails and rescue missions were conducted, all with the specific purpose of communicating the Gospel message to people that desperately needed to hear it. A telephone ministry was initiated to help people move forward in their spiritual journey, and classified newspaper advertising was utilized to build awareness of CBMC-sponsored events.

Hedstrom, who became known for his inspirational messages from the podium, explained how he viewed the mission of CBMC at the time:

"We are only a voice of Him who crieth in the wilderness. Our cry is for God's people to wake up. Christ is coming. Get busy for God.... This unique testimony, that has been so singularly blessed of God, had its beginning here in Chicago. It started in prayer. In fact, it was the result of years of fervent intercessions by several prayer groups which met weekly in several downtown meetings.

"This God-honored and God-sustained testimony can continue only through men who are unselfishly devoted to the cause of Christ, men who are wholly surrendered to God, and who gladly and willingly obey His command and submit to the blueprint of heaven. Surely, if ever God called men to sacrifice to the cause of Christ, it is now."

Speaking at the third convention in 1940, Hedstrom expressed words that could easily describe men involved in CBMC today. "God will bring together a band of men whose hearts He has strangely touched, men who have only one desire and that is to be their best for God, men who will listen to the still, small voice and be ready to go places for Christ."

The United States' entrance into World War II presented CBMC with opportunities to reach out to another segment of American society: the military. This led CBMC to open servicemen's centers for addressing the concerns and fears of soldiers and sailors being deployed, as well as those returning from battle.

By all accounts, CBMC's spiritual outreach to the men in uniform was highly successful. In San Francisco, for example, during its first year of operation, an estimated 116,000 servicemen visited the center, with more than 1,000 of them making professions of faith.

Similar centers were operated in Detroit, New York City, San Diego, Minneapolis, Kansas City, Waukegan, Illinois and other cities. Over a nine-year period, more than 26,000 servicemen indicated they had prayed to invite Jesus Christ into their lives. The centers remained open for several years even after the end of the war. In 1948, the CBMC of Indianapolis, Indiana, founded the Christian Military Men's Committee, which served to sustain the evangelistic focus on servicemen.

While spiritual impact cannot be measured by human statistics, numbers did reflect CBMC's strong commitment to presenting the Gospel of Christ to as many people as possible.

A survey of committee activities in 1947, for example, offered these findings:

Nearly 8,000 open-air, hospital, jail and rescue mission services had been conducted; 625,000 Gospel tracts had been distributed, and more than 30,000 professions of faith had been recorded in the various settings. As David R. Enlow, author of *Men Aflame,* a history of CBMC from its founding through the 1960s, observed, "And this was with only one-fourth of committees reporting, not only in the United States but also in other parts of the world."

Over time, CBMC's international outreach spread to locations such as Pusan, Korea; Cork, Ireland; and Mexico City, Mexico.

A 1950 edition of *Contact,* one of CBMC's early publications, included a statement of CBMC International policy, which described the ministry's methodology at the time. While strategies have changed over time, the heartbeat of CBMC remains the same:

1. *Man-to-man aggressive evangelism.*

2. *Testifying of our life and conduct that Christianity works.*

3. *Demonstrating that Christianity works in business.*

4. *Conducting fellowship activities for the purpose of reaching other men for Christ, such as breakfasts, luncheons and banquets.*

5. *Burnishing and inspiring fellow Christians into a closer fellowship and devotion to Christ.*

6. *Evangelizing as God gives opportunity through open-air and jail meetings, service men's centers, county farms, rescue missions, and even young people's Bible clubs.*

Not included in that list, but just as vital, was a deep commitment to prayer and reliance on God's leading and empowerment. A maxim the early CBMC leaders often cited was, "When you rely on entertainment, you get what entertainment can do; when you rely on personalities, you get what personalities can do; but when you rely on prayer, you get what God will do."

Statements made at annual conventions by many of the founding leaders reflect their passion for serving God and pointing others to the same kind of life-changing encounter with Him that they had experienced.

Many looked to Gremmels as a model of personal evangelism; he continued to share his faith with others well into his 80s. He said, "there are golden opportunities for personal evangelism on trains, buses, taxis, and at stations, hotels and dining places." He was unwavering in his use of Gospel tracts as evangelistic tools.

Grunigen, who was not one of CBMC's founders but was a key to its "western expansion," wrote about the ministry's single-minded purpose: "Active, virile laity will combine to preach the blood of Christ, resist all moves to sidetrack us on reformation projects of one type or another, soft-pedal labels, consolidate our lines in order to unify our efforts in getting the Gospel to as many people as possible in the shortest time possible; joining together with the express intent of waging an assault on godlessness, materialism, unbelief and modernism. What the world needs is the Gospel. Do you like our platform?"

A popular speaker at CBMC events, he often addressed the motivation behind the most zealous CBMC members. In 1953, speaking at a banquet in Tucson, Ariz., Grunigen said, "When you're at the end of yourself, God loves to do things for you. The man who comes to the end of himself and doesn't have Christianity – faith and trust in Jesus Christ – in his heart, that man has no place to go.

"Until we begin to gossip the Gospel, until we begin to tell each other what makes us tick, we haven't lived up to our opportunities in America. [We must be willing] to talk about the great, eternal verities of the Word of God…. It's perfectly ridiculous for preachers, priests, and rabbis to be carrying the whole load. They can't do it. Until butchers, bakers and candlestick makers, stenographers, nurses and all join the group of extroverts who are willing to spread the good news that Christ came to save sinners…until we all do that, the news isn't going to get out."

He added, "Until men are born of God, government and society and philosophy and science will be evil and get worse." More than 60 years after Grunigen made that statement, it seems not much has changed, underscoring that CBMC's holy calling is far from completed.

For many years Waldo Yeager of Toledo, Ohio, was a highly respected leader in CBMC and served as chairman of the CBMCI Board of Directors. The president of the Cortland Produce Company, which raised and processed poultry, he was known as the city's "chicken and egg man."

He had authored a personal tract called "Life's Most Amazing Fact." In this widely used tract, Yeager explained, "There's only one Person who really does know me, and that's God Himself.... He knows *all* about me, and here's the amazing fact – *He still loves me!*"

One of the significant leaders of CBMC during the 1950s was Theodore E. "Theo" McCully, who forged a successful livelihood in the baking business. Like many of his peers, he placed great emphasis on his utter dependence on the Lord for effectiveness and fruitfulness in the ministry.

He observed, "The secret of CBMC continuing on for God to become an even greater power and influence is dependent on each individual member keeping the supply lines open. There is absolutely no substitute for a day-by-day, prayerful meditation on the Word of God."

At another time, McCully wrote about the importance of a daily, abiding relationship with Jesus Christ. "You and I can't live the Christian life. We'll fail every time. It's Christ living in us that enables us to do it."

He held a clear understanding that CBMC was not to be a church, but to serve as an arm of the Church in reaching a segment of society needing to hear the Gospel message in ways that related to their everyday work and challenges.

McCully, who became CBMC's full-time Executive Secretary and worked out of its office in Glen Ellyn, Illinois, stated, "We are not here to duplicate the work of the Bible-believing church.... God has called us as individuals into this CBMC fellowship to present a forceful testimony to the men whom we contact every day in our particular line of business."

On January 5, 1956, McCully suffered a devastating personal loss that was felt not only within the CBMC network, but also throughout the entire Christian community. His son, Ed McCully, was one of five young missionaries killed by Auca Indians in the jungles of Ecuador. Another of the men was Jim Elliot, whose widow, Elisabeth, later wrote a best-selling account of the tragedy – and its triumphant aftermath – in *Through Gates of Splendor,* as well as its sequel, *The Shadow of the Almighty,* and other books.

Just three days after McCully's son's death, revered CBMC leader Arnold Grunigen reflected on the tragic loss with a group of 150 people at a church in Palo Alto, California.

In declining health and despite serious physical limitations, Grunigen said, "Heaven is the goal and hope of the believer. The unsaved person is spending his time, effort and money on earthly habitations. Suppose there was a chance that you could live to be 140, like the man I heard of over in Berkeley who just recently went home to glory....

"I don't know, but even if you did live that long, what is that compared to eternity? Spending eternity with Him is the most glorious thing for the believer.... [The apostle] Paul's immortal hope of glory will be the personal experience of one Arnold Grunigen.... We must be willing to be absent from the body and to be present with the Lord."

As he struggled to complete his message, several times Grunigen repeated the words, "absent...present...it's terrific. I'll be there." About two days later, he passed away and started experiencing the "immortal hope of glory" he so eagerly anticipated.

Despite the grief of losing a son, McCully maintained a rigorous schedule of speaking, carrying out CBMC responsibilities, and other activities. Explaining his capacity for fulfilling such demands at the verge of retirement age, he said, "They that wait upon the Lord shall renew their strength – Isaiah 40:31."

For many years CBMC used the King James translation of Romans 12:11, "not slothful in business, fervent in spirit, serving the Lord" as a motivational slogan. Newer versions would show the original manuscripts were not referring specifically to the business world. The New International Version, for example, translated the passage, "Never be lacking in zeal, but keep your spiritual fervor, serving the Lord." The New American Standard offered the translation, "not lagging behind in diligence, fervent in spirit, serving the Lord." Nevertheless, the passage still challenged many in CBMC to remember their calling to represent Jesus Christ in the marketplace.

Banking executive Harry Smith, who became CBMC's international chairman, acknowledged this in reference to the challenge not only of reaching the lost for Christ, but also in living and working in harmony with fellow believers. He recited a clever little poem that would be oft-quoted in CBMC circles for years to come:

"To live above with saints we love, oh, that will be glory! But to live below with saints we know, well, that's a different story."

By 1960, the total number of CBMC groups in the United States, as well as more than 30 other countries, had grown to more than 500. During that year, six CBMC leaders – at their own expense – traveled to 20 countries in Europe. These including Chairman Waldo Yeager, Vice Chairman Robert Kellogg, and McCully.

The succeeding years marked a time of dramatic changes for the United States. Hawaii had become the 50th state in 1959. Over a span of less than five years, assassinations of three iconic leaders – President John F. Kennedy, his brother, Robert F. Kennedy, and the Rev. Martin Luther King, Jr. – would rock the nation. A part of the world few people knew much about, Southeast Asia, would become front-page news, fueling tremendous national strife and controversy. Social upheaval took on many forms.

Significant change was in the wind for CBMC as well, geographically and philosophically. And by the early 1970s, CBMC would begin redefining and honing its mission, taking steps to pursue Christ's Great Commission more fully.

But its existence – and its legacy – would forever be rooted in its humble, unpretentious beginnings. As Enlow wrote in *Men Aflame*, "Past leaders in CBMC have established a foundation of great treasure upon which you can continue to build your own life, in your family's lives, and in the lives of businessmen around you."

The Billy Graham-CBMC Connection

There's an interesting bit of trivia about how the ministries of CBMC and renowned evangelist Dr. Billy Graham crossed paths, especially in his early days.

In the 1930s, mass evangelism was a popular and effective way of communicating the Gospel to large numbers of people. Billy Sunday, a former professional baseball player turned evangelist, had spoken to millions of people during evangelistic campaigns that spanned more than two decades. But as he entered his 70s, it became evident Sunday's ministry was drawing to a close.

Sensing the need for someone to fill that void, about 25 members of the CBMC of Charlotte, N.C. felt an unusual burden for prayer. Before daylight one morning, they gathered at the farm of a man named William Franklin Graham, Sr. Fasting from sunrise to sunset, they knelt on pine needles in the middle of a grove of pine trees, petitioning God to choose an individual to one day become Sunday's successor.

"What we prayed for," one of the men recalled, "was that the Lord might raise up a man who would take the Gospel to all the world and turn men in far places to Christ. Here we were, praying for such a man, and all the time he was right there on the place."

The "he" referred to was Billy Graham, Frank Graham's son, then 12 years old. At that stage of his life, young Billy had no idea of the mission God had for him in the future. In fact, he is reported to have asked others in his family, "I wonder what those fanatics are doing here?"

Graham did prove to be the answer to the CBMC members' prayers, but that was not the last time he and CBMC would intersect. He was invited to be a guest speaker at the CBMC convention in Kansas City in 1947, while he was still a virtual unknown serving as a vice president with Youth for Christ International.

Then in 1950, early in his crusade ministry, a group consisting primarily of CBMC members sponsored a major evangelistic event in Boston, with Graham the featured evangelist. More than 16,000 people attended the meeting, with thousands more standing outside, unable to enter the packed arena.

One report said, "It was the largest crowd ever to come to Boston Garden, even larger than when Winston Churchill spoke there or when former President (Franklin Delano) Roosevelt was there."

When God called Dr. Graham home in 2018 at the age of 99, he left a sterling legacy of a man who finished well in his service to the Lord. And CBMC celebrated being used by God to help him get started.

In a 1957 interview published in CBMC's *CONTACT* magazine, he said, "The constant support of CBMC from the very beginning of our evangelistic ministry has thrilled and encouraged me beyond words…. CBMC has helped to pioneer in this century a new, but scriptural, emphasis on the laymen's responsibility to the Gospel."

Perspectives on Work and Faith from the 'Dean of Earthmoving'

Robert Gilmour (R.G.) LeTourneau, one of CBMC's early leaders, was a prolific inventor of earthmoving machinery from the 1920s through the 1950s, discovering and implementing technology often years ahead of its time. His expertise earned him the nickname, "The Dean of Earthmoving."

His autobiography, *Mover of Men and Mountains,* spoke of both his business acumen and his passion for serving God and reaching people for Jesus Christ. His financial prosperity enabled him to adopt an unusual practice, a "reverse tithe" – giving 90 percent of his salary and company profits to God's work while keeping only 10 percent for himself.

For more than 30 years, he flew thousands of miles almost weekly for speaking engagements across the United States and around the world.

Clearly a man devoted to the Lord in both business and ministry, LeTourneau died in 1969. Here are some of his observations that reflect his philosophy, faith and perspectives about life:

"By accepting God as your partner, no limit can be placed on what can be achieved."

"I believe that when the Lord comes into a man's heart, it makes him a better workman."

"If the God who is big enough to make a universe is willing to let me be a co-worker with Him, then surely I am not too big to let my men be co-workers with me."

"I try to shovel out more for God than He can for me, but He always wins. He's got a bigger shovel."

"Man's mind is marvelous in its accomplishments, but the human mind falls way short when we try to imagine or understand the goodness of God, His love for us, or His plans for our future."

"The most encouraging sign on the horizon today is the fact businessmen are waking up to their responsibility to God, and beginning to prove that Christianity is practical."

"If you have a guide whom you trust, you don't need to know the destination to take the next step with him."

"...if a person is interested in what they are doing, it ceases to be hard work and becomes more of a game. There is a lot of joy in accomplishment. If more people would learn this secret, they would be happier, and the world would be better off. Then, too, there is the secret of learning what we read in 1 Corinthians 3:9, 'For we are laborers together with God.'"

"I have often made the statement that there is a place where faith leaves off and presumption begins, and I think that accounts for a lot of failures."

Chapter 3

Moving from Death to Life

"He asked me, 'Son of man, can these bones live?' And I answered,
'O Lord God, you know.'" – Ezekiel 37:3

The 1960s and early '70s were exciting, transformative years for the United States, but also very troubled, with grim realities of death dominating news headlines almost daily. The assassinations of President John F. Kennedy, Dr. Martin Luther King, Jr. and Robert F. Kennedy, spanning less than five years, shook the nation. Between 1965 and 1974, more than 58,000 American GIs lost their lives in the Vietnam war, with countless thousands of others returning home scarred physically and emotionally.

But for CBMC, by then an established ministry seeking to sharpen its focus and expand its mission, it wasn't death but life that commanded its attention in several crucial ways.

On the spiritual front, significant strides were being made across the nation. God was using evangelistic crusades, led by the Rev. Billy Graham and others, to touch the lives of countless thousands in many segments of society. Ministries were starting to proliferate for families, children, the poor, and even for those on college campuses.

At the same time, however, America's shift toward secularization was gaining traction. Judeo-Christian values and traditions were undergoing serious attack in many levels of society, including government, entertainment, the media, and commerce.

It was the business and professional world that would receive CBMC's focus, since spiritual needs of people in the marketplace were largely being overlooked, if not ignored. Some in the Christian world had concluded that because of their material success and power, men in the marketplace were largely "unreachable."

CBMC's national board members disagreed. They knew firsthand that such individuals were as spiritually bankrupt as anyone, and after hearing the Good News of Jesus Christ from someone with whom they could relate, often would respond both positively and enthusiastically.

For this reason, the board determined to redefine CBMC from a network of businessmen striving to address a spectrum of spiritual needs to a more narrow mission: presenting the Gospel message specifically to unsaved business and professional men and helping new believers grow in their faith.

Paul Johnson, a successful building contractor in Detroit, Michigan, was one of them. He had started college intending to become an architect, but had gotten a job with a contractor for practical work experience. After what he described as becoming "acquainted with bricks and two-by-fours," Johnson discovered his vocational passion was to build rather than to design. He started constructing houses, then moved to commercial projects such as factories, hospitals, schools, airport terminals, apartments and office buildings.

Johnson was introduced to CBMC in 1954 when John Boyko, a man he had known casually through church, invited him to a weekend men's retreat at a lake setting near Fenton, about an hour's drive from Detroit. All the speakers at the retreat were businessmen, including Stanley Kresge, son of S.S. Kresge, founder of the Kresge "dime stores" that later became the Kmart Corporation.

Boyko continued inviting Johnson to other CBMC meetings, and he eventually found it a comfortable fit. "I learned the purpose of the organization was to encourage Christian men to share their faith and the Gospel of Jesus Christ with other men through luncheons or dinners where businessmen gave their testimonies," he said.

"I enjoyed the meetings very much, and was encouraged by hearing other men speak about Christian growth and their walk with the Lord. I was only about 26 at the time, and all these older men encouraged me to always put the Lord first in my life, and that I did not need to be ashamed or timid about my faith."

Johnson became active in CBMC locally, serving on the area's CBMC board and becoming chairman of the Detroit committee. With his wife, Marilyn, he started attending annual national conventions, and after several years, was elected to succeed Boyko as a member of CBMC's national board of directors.

One of Johnson's board responsibilities was to visit 17 local CBMC committees in Michigan and Ohio at least once a year, offering encouragement and assistance. The board members, each assigned to oversee a district in the part of the country where they lived and worked, would try to provide some direction. However, being volunteers, they had limited time for providing actual training in ministry strategies.

"It became a part-time job," Johnson said. "I already had a full-time job, but it was a real joy. I saw men from all walks of life come to faith in Christ through the lives and testimonies of other Christian businessmen. It was a very fulfilling experience to see men's lives changed, marriages restored, families reunited with a new purpose in life, and about every good thing you could think of.

"I got into the ministry with both feet. I went from being encouraged to being an encourager. I loved our theme Bible verse, Romans 12:11, which in the old King James Version reads, 'Diligent in business, fervent in spirit, serving the Lord.'"

Dedication and passion, however, could only go so far. By this time, CBMC had grown to nearly 500 groups gathering across the country. Like Johnson, the other 16 national board members realized it was impossible for them to consistently visit each of their groups to provide needed support and challenge the men in the ministry.

Theo McCully, CBMC's longtime executive secretary, had retired. Nearly a dozen staff people had been hired to carry out various responsibilities at the CBMC central office in Glen Ellyn, Illinois, a Chicago suburb, including maintaining communications with groups and individuals from coast to coast.

In 1974, John Shoop, a veteran CBMC member who had held management positions with a company in nearby Elgin, Illinois, was brought on as executive vice president to oversee daily operations in Glen Ellyn. But there was no one to serve as a standard bearer, a spokesman to promote the mission and vision of CBMC from coast to coast. The national board determined to find a president to provide this leadership.

John Bruehl of Normal, Illinois was the board's initial choice, a longtime CBMC member with an evangelistic heart and a sensitive demeanor. He assumed the new role in 1975. However, because the position was both part-time and unpaid, Bruehl found himself needing to devote most of his time to managing the independent auto glass and tire companies he had established.

At the same time, the national board had been seeking God's wisdom and guidance as they continued to evaluate what CBMC needed in a president long-term. Ted DeMoss, an insurance executive who had been involved with the ministry for about 25 years and had served on the board as a national field representative, emerged as a favored candidate to succeed Bruehl.

DeMoss had been introduced to CBMC in the mid-1950s by his older cousin, Art DeMoss, who also had gotten Ted started in the insurance business. (*More about how Ted became involved with CBMC in chapter 4.*)

A former military pilot, Ted operated several regional insurance offices in the Southeast and would fly his company plane to the different locations. He was already using the plane to travel around the country to personally visit with CBMC groups and speak at outreach functions. This enabled him to avoid the time constraints of commercial air travel and often made it possible to visit multiple cities in a matter of a few days, or even a single day.

Once the national board determined in 1976 that he was God's choice to lead CBMC across the country as President, one obstacle remained. DeMoss had been born and raised in upstate New York, but had moved to Chattanooga, Tennessee. With his wife and three daughters, they had established deep roots there and had no interest in relocating to Chicago and the Midwest.

CBMC's operations had been based in Chicago since its founding in 1930, so to consider moving its central office constituted a "big discussion," according to Paul Johnson, who was serving on the national board at the time. "It was a milestone decision, going from Chicago to Chattanooga. But we eventually came to the conclusion that it did not matter where the CBMC office was," he said.

A handful of staff members were willing to relocate to Tennessee; others were given assistance in pursuing new employment opportunities.

The next question regarded where in Chattanooga to establish CBMC's "nerve center," and this was where the answer provided an ironic juxtaposition of death and life.

Paul Martin, a Christian counselor, and DeMoss attended church together. One Sunday Ted was telling him about becoming the new CBMC President and the decision to relocate the ministry's offices to Chattanooga. Martin had just learned owners of the Chattanooga Funeral Home, which maintained several sites around the city, were wanting to sell their building on McCallie Avenue, so he asked Ted whether he thought that might be suitable for CBMC's needs.

The facility offered the potential for 18,000 square feet of office space over three stories, including a large auditorium space, along with a garage area and parking for 80 cars. The facility's price tag was $250,000 – $200,000 for the structure and $50,000 for renovations.

Funding for the purchase and remodeling came from several sources. The Kresge Foundation in Troy, Michigan provided a grant of $50,000, and two Chattanooga business leaders – Scott Probasco, then president of American National Bank, a local financial institution, and Hugh O. Maclellan, Sr., founder of Provident Insurance Company – were instrumental in raising the additional funds.

Larry Kendrick, who had been hired by Shoop late in 1977 to assist with administrative responsibilities, was among staff who relocated from Glen Ellyn to Chattanooga. He was given the task of handling logistics for the physical move.

"A couple of foundations really believed in Ted and donated a large sum to buy the old funeral parlor. Financially, it was a choice between moving to Chattanooga and owning the property outright, with no rent, or continuing to pay rent in Chicago for 1,400 square feet," Kendrick said, observing that both the economics and the desire to have DeMoss assume CBMC's top leadership role made the decision a relatively simple one for the national board.

Not All of the Bodies Were Buried

The irony of a ministry dedicated to pointing business and professional men to Jesus Christ and eternal life relocating to a building that had housed a business devoted to the disposition of the dead was obvious, Kendrick said.

"While we were moving in and doing renovations, there were still coffins in the hallways, caskets were still being displayed in the basement, and the inside of the building was in considerable disrepair. Wallpaper was peeling off the walls. In the basement was also a garage, and limousines and hearses were still being parked there."

Kendrick recalled a time when Shoop was in the basement and heard a phone ring in a room nearby, where he knew bodies were still being prepared for burial. When he walked around a corner to answer the phone, a man stepped out of the room toward him. It took Shoop more than a few moments to recover from that "surprise," not realizing a staff person from the funeral home had been performing his duties in there.

Gene Johnson had been hired to work part-time in CBMC's Glen Ellyn offices, handling the distribution of ministry materials such as the "10 Most Wanted" card and outreach registration cards. As one of those who had agreed to move to Chattanooga, he interfaced directly with the movers and people hired locally to carry furnishings and equipment into the Chattanooga site. He recalled another incident underscoring the "death to life" contrast.

Along with caskets that had not yet been removed from the basement, an embalming table was still there. The building's custodian, Bruce Cobb, had been doing some cleanup work, and Johnson was directing students from nearby Tennessee Temple University who had been hired to unload the moving trucks. One day while furniture was being brought into the building, Cobb and Johnson decided to pull an innocent prank.

Cobb went down to the basement, laid down on the embalming table and draped a sheet over himself. On cue, Johnson brought two of the students into the room. "I said to them, 'Can you believe this? There's still a body in there.' As we entered, Bruce dropped one of his arms from under the sheet. When the students saw that, their eyes got really big and they ran out of the building, not looking back. We never did see them again!"

Johnson, who later assumed a full-time staff role as materials and promotions manager for CBMC, continued to manifest his unique sense of humor there for nearly 20 years.

From Darkness to Light

While CBMC was adapting to a new home, mission and leadership, God was continuing to do an unusual work in the life of a young man more than 1,200 miles away. A longtime resident of Pierre, South Dakota, Ken Korkow was in the midst of what many would have considered a charmed life. He had survived numerous brushes with death, built a highly successful career in real estate, and was experiencing prosperity that most people could only imagine. Then a contractor he was dealing with asked a few simple questions, turning Ken's life upside-down.

Ten years earlier, success and prosperity had been a faint hope for Ken, if that. While many of his peers were listening to the Beatles, living hippie lifestyles, staging peace protests and carrying signs reading, "Make love not war," Ken had left college after two years to enlist in the U.S. Marines. Rather than opposing the war, he was eager to join the fighting in Vietnam.

Working in the family's rodeo and ranching operations in Pierre had shaped his rough-and-tumble approach to life, and he looked forward to engaging in combat. When orders deploying to Vietnam weren't forthcoming, Ken even appealed to U.S. Sen. George McGovern of South Dakota for help in persuading the Marines to permit him to defend his country.

Soon after arriving for duty in Southeast Asia, it became apparent Ken was cut from a different cloth than many of his Marine colleagues. They were willing to fight but anxious to leave, but he was fearless. He even came to regard the war as "fun."

"If you had asked me back then, I would have told you that I don't get scared or cry. I scare others and make others cry. It may sound strange, even inhumane to say it now, but while I was in Vietnam, I was filled with so much hate that I enjoyed killing people. For someone who has never fought in a war, that may not make sense, but even for those who were there, I was extreme," he admitted. "There was no greater glory than fighting in battle. For me, combat was a life-sized adventure.

"I used to volunteer for patrols and sneak out, looking for trouble. One time a patrol went out and I wasn't allowed to go with it. Out of the 40-plus Marines that went out, 27 were killed. Everyone else was wounded, including one who was a prisoner of war for over five years."

That was just the first of many near-death experiences Ken would have. Three times he had been knocked down by the concussion of mortar explosions without suffering injury, but was not as fortunate during the 1968 Tet offensive, in the highly publicized siege of Khe Sanh.

In a clearing between the two fighting forces, bodies of dead Marines had lain for more than a month. Ken was a point man for one of two groups that went out in a coordinated effort to retrieve the bodies of their comrades, holding true to the motto, "no Marine left behind." During the recovery effort, he was hit by blasts from three 61-millimeter mortar shells.

"They had gotten me good. I could not move my arms and legs. I was a bloody mess. Two guys came out to get me and miraculously, in the middle of intense combat, we passed between the gun and mortar fire without suffering another scratch. We huddled for safety in a huge B-52 bomb crater where two medical corpsmen and a doctor were attending to the wounded. They provided my initial first aid."

Ken was airlifted out of the war zone and taken to a military hospital for treatment and convalescence. His heroics would eventually earn him the prestigious Navy Cross, ranked second in importance only to the Congressional Medal of Honor, but that was of little concern as he determined to prove his doctors wrong by overcoming his battlefield disabilities.

When he had recovered sufficiently to return home, Ken got back in the saddle as soon as he could at the family ranch, even though his normal walk had been reduced to a hobble. It wasn't long before he added to his growing list of harrowing encounters.

One day he and one of the ranch hands were riding trained quarter horses to round up the ranch's stock of bulls in a pasture of more than 1,000 acres. All the bulls, except for a Mexican fighting bull, had been corralled. That one suddenly charged and gored Ken's horse, mortally wounding it. Getting off the dying horse, he knew he would be the bull's next target. Still far from healed of his injuries, chances of eluding the vicious bull in the vast pasture were extremely slim.

"My only asset was that in the rodeo business you learn how to deal with bulls, and I had learned well the Marine Corps philosophy that you never give up your life. If someone wants it, he'll have to work for it," he commented.

As he tried to devise an evasive strategy, the bull was about twenty feet away and quickened its pace from a determined walk to a trot. For Ken, running was not a viable option. Suddenly, just eight feet away, the animal stopped, cocked its head to one side, then turned and retreated to another part of the pasture.

"I really couldn't understand why the bull did that, but didn't wait around to figure it out. Once I got out of the pasture, I got onto another horse and with another ranch hand, we went back for the bull."

One year after the incident with the bull, he was the announcer at a rodeo when a boy was thrown from a horse and knocked unconscious. For some moments the youngster had stopped breathing, but was resuscitated by paramedics and taken to a nearby hospital. The next day, Ken had a similar accident when one of the broncs he was sorting crashed into him, slamming him to the ground. His brother, Jim, happened to come around the corner and spot him lying motionless, not breathing.

The brother's first thought was, "Ken's dead," but help quickly arrived. He was revived and transported for treatment. Ken awakened in a hospital room next to the young rodeo victim, both living to tell about their extremely close calls.

Seeming to have become a human counterpart of the "cat with nine lives," he wasn't finished keeping death at a mere arm's length. The following summer, he and his wife, Liz, began taking parachute lessons. Weather conditions were marginal because of the low cloud level, but they determined to make their jumps.

Liz went first and got out of the plane cleanly, but as he prepared for his turn, Ken looked below and began having misgivings. But with his wife already descending, he wasn't about to back out, so he jumped.

Once his parachute opened, Ken realized he was heading toward a clump of trees. He managed to maneuver around the trees, but snagged a power line instead. Once again, this man who virtually knew death on a first-name basis, escaped injury. It seemed like he had a personal guardian angel assigned to him, working overtime.

These and other episodes were not forgotten, and in 1978 were brought to clear focus during the conversation with the contractor, Jim Stokes. At that point in his life, Ken had discovered a natural affinity for real estate development and investment. "I could touch manure and it would turn into gold," he recalled years later.

Rewards for his business success included a 15-room, 6,000 square foot house that was under construction, with an accompanying 4,000-square foot garage with eight automobile stalls. He envisioned a Rolls Royce filling one of the spaces.

After finishing their business discussions, Stokes had shifted gears and asked Ken several pointed questions about life – eternal life – and Jesus Christ.

"He asked me if I believed in God, and I told him I did. He then asked if I believed in Jesus Christ and the Bible. I told him yes, that I had even been active in my church as a youth. Lastly, he asked me if I had ever committed my life to Jesus Christ as Savior and Lord. Then he showed me a few verses in the Bible that said that everyone has sinned, that the wages of sin is death, and that the free gift of God is eternal life for all who know Jesus Christ.

"Then something strange happened – I got scared. I wanted to get out of Jim's house, away from him. I was a tough person. I had killed many people in war, so I wasn't accustomed to being afraid. But if a person could really 'know that you have eternal life,' as one of the verses said – and I didn't – that meant I was on the outside, separated from God and headed for hell."

Stokes had written down references to the verses so Ken could read them again later, and he did. "As I read them, I saw there was no way they could be taken out of context. As I read these passages, I knew I was a sinner, and I clearly saw the penalty for sin is death. Thinking of my past, I realized how many times God had spared me from death, even at times when men who were nicer and more deserving were killed. I remembered Vietnam, the fighting bull, and other near misses, but that was the first time I ever thought about how God had protected me."

As he pondered this, Ken also realized that despite all the trappings of success, the goals he had achieved and the things he possessed, he had never experienced true, lasting happiness.

"That came as quite a shock. For only the second or third time since Vietnam, I cried. I called out to a God I really didn't know. I said, 'I don't know who or what You are, but I've made a mess of my life. All these things should have made me happy, but my life is empty.'"

After praying for forgiveness and agreeing to turn his life over to God, he paused, not knowing what to expect. "I don't know what I was waiting for. I guess I expected the National Anthem, the Marine Corps Hymn, the hairs on the back of my neck to stand up, the earth to shake, or maybe see an angel jump onto the mantle. But nothing happened. Then I broke down sobbing, reasoning that although I believed God could forgive sin, I was such a bad sinner that He would not forgive me."

After a restless, sleepless night, he decided to call someone who might be able to answer his troubling questions. Because he did not know Stokes other than as a business acquaintance, instead Ken called Gene Reed, a banker he had befriended through his business dealings. Reed was active in CBMC in Pierre, although at that point Ken had no idea what CBMC was.

"I remembered from talking with Gene that he seemed to know a lot about the Bible. When I called and told him I wanted to talk about Christianity, he replied, 'Praise the Lord!' My immediate thought was, 'Oh, no. Not one of those.' But as I talked with him, I realized Gene wasn't a fanatic, but someone who had a firm grip on who he was and where he was going in his life. After I told him what had happened the previous day, Gene gave me some excellent advice. He explained that to be a Christian, you can't place your faith in an experience. Your faith has to be based on the truth of God's Word, the Bible."

Reed introduced Ken to Jim Kienholz, a local engineer, and for the next year they met weekly in a one-to-one Bible study called *Operation Timothy*. Kienholz and Reed also introduced him to CBMC. "There I met a lot of guys who had a sincere faith in Jesus Christ and made Him an integral part of their lives. I had a lot of rough edges, but these guys showed a genuine love for me in spite of it all."

Several months later, after attending a CBMC couples' dinner, his wife, Liz, also committed her life to Christ. Together they have been on an exciting but unpredictable journey of faith ever since.

Not long after becoming a follower of Jesus, Ken's business career suffered a dramatic reversal. "After so many years of seemingly turning manure into gold, it seemed that if I touched gold it would turn into manure," he said.

Financial struggles taught the Korkows difficult but unforgettable, undeniable lessons about God's faithfulness and timely provision. They learned the importance of realigning their priorities around the Lord and principles He presents in the Scriptures. And they began to invest in others spiritually just as people had been doing with them.

On April 1, 1984 – April Fool's Day, Ken likes to point out – he joined the staff of CBMC, becoming a staff Director in Omaha, Nebraska, and has been to this day. Over more than three decades, he and the team that has developed in Omaha, Lincoln and other communities in the region have ministered to men and their families, sharing the same Good News that forever changed their own lives.

He also has used his CBMC training and experiences in several other ministries, including the Post Traumatic Growth Institute, which enables him to work closely with other war veterans who discovered they were suffering from post-traumatic stress disorder (PTSD).

For years, Ken didn't realize he was a sufferer of PTSD, even though he exhibited many of its common symptoms. Being engaged in warfare and seeing death in the most intense, horrific way left emotional wounds that dwarfed the physical scars he still bears today. But through God's transforming power, and what he learned through CBMC, he is helping other PTSD victims learn to shift their focus from death and understand for the first time what real life – eternal life – is all about.

In the next chapter, we'll look at the very different, but equally powerful story of God's transforming work in another businessman, Ted DeMoss.

Chapter 4 –

A New Face for the Ministry

"Then I heard the voice of the Lord, saying, 'Whom shall I send, and who will go for Us?' Then I said, 'Here am I. Send me!' " – Isaiah 6:8

Do you remember "Columbo"? He was the TV detective, portrayed by Peter Falk, who typically arrived on the scene in a rumpled raincoat, looking anything but an astute sleuth who could deftly sort through random clues to solve a heinous crime. In a sense, Ted DeMoss, who served as President of CBMC-USA from 1977 to 1991, gave that initial Columbo-type of impression.

A popular outreach speaker for CBMC for many years, even before and after his tenure as President, Ted would open his talks in a straight-forward but unassuming manner that might have caused first-time guests to wonder, "Who is this guy?" However, within minutes he held his audience in rapt attention, listening to heartfelt words from a man whose greatest passions were Jesus Christ and reaching out to those who didn't yet know Him.

Ted would share part of his own spiritual journey, incorporating recent stories about people he had encountered who had been struggling with various personal dilemmas. The focus of his messages was always on Jesus and what He could do to give people peace, hope, deliverance from whatever dire straits they were facing, and most all, assurance of life after their time on earth came to an end.

Regarded by some as the greatest one-on-one evangelist they had ever known, Ted didn't rely on polished rhetorical techniques when he spoke, hundreds of times a year. With an unpretentious manner, he simply related what he often termed "the best news in life."

When asked to explain his strategy for conducting an evangelistic outreach meeting, he would respond it was essentially the equivalent of "one beggar telling another beggar where he could find some bread."

During his early adult years, however, no one – including himself – could have guessed Ted would end up devoting decades of his life talking with people about where they would be spending eternity, and what a personal relationship with Jesus Christ would mean for their everyday lives.

He was raised by Greek immigrants whose last name had been Americanized from Demosthenes to DeMoss. Ted would quip that his father, a jeweler in Albany, New York, "only worked half a day – 12 hours." His dad didn't attend church for the first 45 years of Ted's life, and his mother rarely attended, only on holidays like Christmas and Easter.

"My father never mentioned them, but I was convinced there was a God, a heaven, and a hell. I somehow knew they existed. But one question bothered me more than anything else in the world: Who goes where?" he often explained in giving his testimony.

"I came to the conclusion that if you're good, you go to heaven, and if you're bad, you go to hell. So, I tried to live a good life. I really made an effort to walk the way I thought God would want me to walk," he said. "As a young man I even started attending Sunday school and church, which was strange since my parents didn't go.

"I didn't know one church from another, so I picked a big, name-brand church and attended it for a number of years. I eventually joined the church, had water put on my head and got my own box of envelopes, but still didn't know one thing about whether I would go to heaven or hell."

That changed one day, not in a sanctuary but at an evangelistic meeting. Ted heard the speaker explain, "'it is not good people who go to heaven and bad people who go to hell. Simply because there aren't any good people.' He pointed out that every man and woman alive has broken every one of the Ten Commandments, in thought, word or deed. He said there is one thing that separates people from God, and that is sin. We've all sinned, we've all missed the mark. He then pointed out that the Bible said God made Jesus Christ to be sin for us, and since Christ had no sin of His own, we could have the righteousness of God through Him.

"That night, by faith I accepted God's provision for my sin through Jesus Christ – I lost my religion and began a relationship. I came to realize that religion and Christianity are entirely different. Religion, according to the dictionary, is man's best effort to find God. Christianity is the opposite: God's best effort to find man. You spell religion with two letters: 'Do!' Christianity is spelled with four letters: 'Done.'"

This became the message Ted communicated many thousands of times over more than four decades. Almost immediately, he began a lifelong habit of reading the Bible daily, but would not begin sharing his faith with others until years later.

"After I had finished repeating the sinner's prayer, the speaker offered the best counsel any new believer can be given. He said as a Christian, I should read God's Word every day. For some reason I never questioned that suggestion, and I have been reading the Scriptures on a daily basis for more than forty years," he wrote in his book, *The Gospel and the Briefcase*.

This proved especially helpful, Ted explained, because at the time he wasn't attending a strong, Bible-teaching church. "The only thing that kept me from getting into deep sin was the daily feeding I received directly from the Word of God."

He maintained this practice while serving as a U.S. Navy pilot during World War II, which set him apart from his fellow flyers. "I was the only member of my squadron who took out the Bible each day and read it. I received a lot of ribbing about it, but perhaps God gave me a thick skin so I could ignore my critics and keep on reading."

Ted took to heart what he read, seeking to apply it to every area of his life. Upon encountering the admonition to avoid becoming "unequally yoked" (2 Corinthians 6:14), he said it "literally leaped out at me that I must marry a Christian girl." When he met and started dating Edith Futch, while he was in pre-flight training at the University of North Carolina, he made certain she fit that qualification.

Early in their relationship, they began reading the Bible and praying together, and before long Ted realized he had discovered his life partner. As his wife, Edith not only became the mother of their three daughters, June, Edie and Gwynne, but also accompanied him on many CBMC ministry trips across the country and around the world.

After his wartime service, Ted left the Navy to resume his college education, which he had started at Renssalaer Polytechnic Institute in Troy, New York. While studying there, he maintained his flying credentials, which would prove invaluable to his business career, and later when he assumed a variety of CBMC leadership roles.

He also stayed committed to reading the Scriptures every day, making it part of his personal "curriculum" at Renssalaer. During his senior year, Ted was asked to serve as a teaching assistant for an advanced cost accounting class, working with a highly regarded professor on campus. They spent a lot of time together, and this relationship provided a pivotal moment that helped to shape Ted's perspective on life and ministry.

"The professor was an excellent educator, he was good-looking and young, in his late 30s. He had inherited money from a relative, which enabled him to drive the biggest Lincoln available and buy the loveliest home of any of the teachers I knew," Ted recalled. "He became my ideal. I concluded it would be great to be rich, intelligent, popular, and know as much about as many subjects as he did.

"One winter evening we stayed up late grading papers in his office, and afterward trudged in the deep snow toward our respective homes. Shortly before we parted company at his house, he said something that stunned me: 'Ted, I've come to the conclusion that nothing in life makes any sense.' I didn't know how to respond, so I feebly inquired if he had ever tried 'religion.' My revered professor replied he had studied all the major religions of the world on site, spending his summers traveling all over the world to find out what people believed and why they believed it. When I asked if he had ever considered Christianity, he commented he had looked at that, too.

"Here was a man who, in my mind, had it all. Yet he had just stated quite plainly that 'nothing in life makes any sense.' In June I graduated with a degree in management engineering, but that talk remained fresh in my mind. The next fall, on the opening day of school, my friend – the professor – took his life.

"I will never forget looking at his body in the casket and thinking, 'Some preacher is going to have to pay for not getting the Gospel to this man.' I had been with him on literally hundreds of occasions, yet it never occurred to me that I had any responsibility for sharing my own faith with him.

"I left the funeral home devastated. The man who had everything now had nothing. I was very troubled that someone had not introduced him to Jesus Christ, but at the time failed to realize the role I could have played."

After graduating from Renssalaer, Ted entered a management training program at the Arrow Shirt Company's largest plant in Troy. While still in the program, only 23 years old, he was given responsibility for all shirt manufacturing. This meant he oversaw the work of 550 people, with a management team reporting to him.

The plant was producing 10,000 dozen shirts a week, and he worked with engineers, quality control people, foremen, machinists and sewing machine operators. He was even involved in labor union negotiations. It was an ideal opportunity for a new college graduate, but after nearly two years, Ted typed a letter of resignation. He hadn't even discussed this with Edith, but hand-carried the letter to the plant's front office.

Upon reading the letter, the shocked plant manager asked Ted why he wanted to leave. "I told him, 'Frankly, I'm not sure why I'm leaving. All I know is that I can't give my life to making shirts.'"

The plant manager asked what he planned to do, and Ted admitted he had no plans. Tearing up the letter and throwing it into a wastebasket, the manager told Ted to take a few days off to reconsider. He said the company would not accept the resignation of such a promising young leader.

Ted took some time off, then resumed working for several months until he again walked into the plant manager's office, determined to leave the company without having any idea what his future held. Despite attempts to persuade him to stay, Ted clung to his conviction that there had to be more to work – and life – than making shirts. He did leave, even though he and Edith had little in financial reserves.

Over the next weeks, he interviewed for jobs in the United States, as well as several foreign countries, but none sparked his interest. Without a job or income, Ted faced a major predicament until his cousin, Art DeMoss, approached him about selling insurance. At first Ted resisted the idea, but with no other options finally agreed to give it a try.

Soon he found himself making as much money in a single week as he had earned over an entire month at the shirt company, but still felt all he had really done was exchange making shirts for selling insurance. "I could not help but wonder what God wanted me to do with my life," he recalled. Then God began to reveal His answer – through a ministry called CBMC.

Ted's cousin was a fairly new believer who had become involved with a CBMC group in Albany. Art invited Ted to a CBMC prayer meeting, where he observed men who prayed faithfully for unsaved men by name. The impact on Ted was life-changing, giving him a vision for what the Lord might have in mind for him.

"They talked to me about reaching people for Christ. I responded something like, 'That's not our job,' adding I thought the job of Christian businessmen was to make money and put it into the offering plate so the preachers could win the lost to Christ. I could not have been further from the truth.

"My first reaction was that these had to be the craziest guys I had ever known, praying for hundreds of men and planning to invite many of them to a dinner at our finest hotel where a businessman would tell them how he met Jesus Christ."

Without bringing a guest himself, Ted attended that outreach dinner and had his preconceptions shattered. After the guest speaker presented a simple testimony about his relationship with Jesus, Ted saw several men pray to give their lives to the Lord.

"I had been a Christian for several years, but at the age of 25, for the first time I saw someone converted. These men showed me that if I started to pray for men who did not know Jesus Christ, and then shared the Good News with them, I could see some of my friends come to Christ."

They gave Ted some tips on how to effectively share his faith, and told him to pray daily that God would make him sensitive to the needs of people around him, asking the Lord to provide guidance when he was supposed to speak to someone about Christ. His first real opportunity was not a friend. It was a complete stranger, and the encounter was as unlikely as he could have imagined.

One day he went to an apartment building to respond to a direct mail sales lead. The man inside the third-floor apartment didn't seem interested in having a visitor, especially someone he didn't know, but eventually Ted persuaded him to open the door.

"The referral card had indicated the man might be interested in talking about insurance, but when he opened the door, I saw there was no point in that. It was a man with a white beard who looked like Santa Claus, except he was very thin. I hadn't been in the business that long, but knew he was too old for insurance. I later learned he was 81 years old."

Ted sensed God might have him there for another reason, so he told the man he simply wanted to talk with him. "The only thing that came to my mind was, 'I want to read the Bible to you.' I had absolutely no preparation, but my CBMC friends had told me about using the third chapter of John.

"The fellow responded, 'Go ahead,' but I didn't have a Bible with me, so I asked if he had one. 'I don't know whether I have a Bible or not. I'm blind,' he said. I had not even noticed he was blind!"

After a brief search, Ted found a Bible atop a stack of books, covered with dust. He took it back to the couch where the man was sitting, opened it and began slowly reading chapter three of the Gospel of John.

"I never looked at him as I read. In fact, the further I read, the more scared I got because I couldn't remember what I should do next. I read slower and slower until I got to verse 18, 'He who believes in Him is not judged; he who does not believe has been judged already, because he has not believed in the name of the only begotten Son of God.'

"As I finished that verse, I prayed for the Lord to give me wisdom as to what I should do. I looked over at the old man and saw his beard was wet with tears because of what he had just heard from the Bible. I wasn't trained, but still had enough sense to realize God had indeed spoken to this man through His Word.

"I asked the man, 'Sir, would you like to invite Jesus Christ into your life now, right here?' He said, 'Well, I would like to do it right now, but not right here.' 'Where do you want to go?' I asked him. 'I want to do it with my mother,' was his reply.

"Mentally I was scratching my head. The man had told me he was 81 years old, so I wondered, *what do I say now?* I decided to ask, 'Where is your mother?' 'In the kitchen,' he said. Okay, I supposed there probably was a picture of her in the kitchen, and he wanted to go in there for sentimental reasons. But to my surprise, when we got to the kitchen, there was his mother. She was 98 years old and an invalid, sitting in a canvas-backed chair.

"I've never forgotten the man's words when he told her, 'Mother, God has sent a man to our home. He's been reading the Bible to me, and I'm going to accept Jesus Christ.'

"I don't believe I have ever heard a woman scream like she did. They probably heard her all the way down on the first floor. When she regained control of her emotions, the aged woman told me an amazing thing: 'Mister, I don't know who you are, but I have prayed for my boy every day for over 80 years. I knew Jesus Christ as my personal Savior when my son was born, and I've prayed for him all these years.'

"We got on our knees, and I had the joy of praying with him and seeing him come to Jesus Christ. God had answered two prayers: hers of 80 years, and mine of just a few weeks!'"

That was how Ted got started in the work of CBMC, launching him on an impassioned evangelistic journey that continued for the rest of his life. Over the succeeding years he settled into the "temporary" job his cousin, Art, had given him and it proved to be a suitable vocation. In 1951 he and his family moved to Chattanooga, Tennessee, where he built an insurance business that grew to 19 offices in five states.

He was becoming increasingly involved with CBMC as well, first locally and then as a member of the National Board of Directors. He also served as president of Fishers of Men, a ministry based in the Southeast with a similar mission to CBMC, and the two merged in 1960. He became a much-in-demand outreach speaker, not only communicating the Gospel in his unique, humble manner, but also using his own story to challenge and inspire others to become more proactive in reaching out to people who needed to hear the saving message of Christ.

One friend recalled the singular passion Ted had for sharing his faith in Jesus Christ wherever he went. One time, while on a ministry trip to South Africa, Ted was asked to join a group on a safari tour. Rather than anticipating the opportunity to see wild game, such as lions, elephants and zebras, he had one question: "Will there be people there I can talk with about the Lord?"

True to his calling, every night during the tour in the game preserve, he went from tent to tent, talking about the Gospel of Christ with anyone who would listen.

When he succeeded John Bruehl and became CBMC's first full-time President in 1977, Ted was instrumental in refining CBMC's focus on the business and professional world. Under his leadership, a number of key innovations were introduced to the ministry, some of which will be discussed in the following chapter. They included:

- Office Visitation, a novel strategy for following up on guests in their offices after an outreach event.

- Use of *Steps to Peace With God*, an evangelistic tract, as a primary follow-up tool for helping non-believers understand what a commitment to Jesus Christ means.

- The "Ten Most Wanted" card, which CBMC members in hundreds of weekly prayer meetings have used as handy reminders to pray for unsaved friends, colleagues and customers by name.

- Life-changing discipling tools such as *First Steps* and *Operation Timothy*, following the admonition of 2 Timothy 2:2 to engage in spiritual multiplication and discipleship.

- Creation of a unique on-campus outreach ministry at Auburn University, patterned after CBMC, working with his grandchildren, Joseph and Jennifer Wingfield.

After Ted was succeeded as President of CBMC in 1990 by Phil Downer, he remained on the National Board for six more years. During that time, he continued to serve as an outreach speaker and also helped in furthering CBMC's mission to present Jesus Christ as Savior and Lord to business and professional men, and develop Christian business and professional men to carry out the Great Commission.

Even though God worked through Ted in powerful ways for many years, not only in CBMC but also helping to support other Christian ministries and causes, he often would say of himself, "I'm nothing special." Despite being known from coast to coast, and in many parts of the world, for his evangelistic messages, he never lost sight of how God in His grace had touched his life and how utterly dependent he was on the Lord to participate fruitfully in a unique ministry to the marketplace.

In 2 Timothy 4:7 the apostle Paul wrote, "I have fought the good fight, I have finished the race, I have kept the faith." That is what Ted did, quite literally.

In October 1997 he had flown to California, where he served as guest speaker at more than a dozen CBMC outreach meetings in eight different cities, including Fresno, Sacramento and San Francisco. Dozens of people responded to his messages. Several days later, on Oct. 31, three days before his unexpected death on Nov. 3, he traveled to Knoxville, Tennessee to speak to more than 600 men and women at the city's Mayor's Prayer Breakfast. At the close, approximately 150 people marked cards indicating first-time commitments to Christ.

Bill Yoder, one of the leaders for CBMC in Knoxville at the time, commented, "I had heard Ted speak many times before, but I don't know how his talk could have been any better. It was powerful, and God used him mightily.

"Actually, Ted began ministering the night before when he met with about a dozen of us to pray for the breakfast and challenge us to be faithful in following up on those who would respond."

Many times, Ted would close his talks with a brief poem, accentuating his deep desire to be used by God to communicate the saving message of Jesus Christ to anyone willing to hear it:

"When in the mansions above,
The saved all around us appear,
I must hear someone say,
'It was you who invited me here.'"

The legacy of Ted DeMoss lives on today, more than two decades after the Lord called him home and certainly welcomed him with the words, "Well done, good and faithful servant."

Consider the unlikely beginnings: A deep-seated conviction that there was a God, a heaven and a hell, accompanied by a diligent search to answer the question, "Who goes where?" The suicide of a beloved professor who had seemed to have everything, but from an eternal perspective had nothing. Introduction to a group of faithful men who believed in praying for the salvation of people who didn't know Jesus Christ. And an 81-year-old blind man whose still-living mother had been praying for his eternal destiny for more than 80 years.

God used each of those moments in Ted's life to instill a passion for the lost that served to inspire countless others to use their own jobs and companies as platforms for reaching other business and professional men for Christ, and helping believers to grow in their faith so they in turn could reach others.

In the following chapter, we'll look at some of those strategies, many of which remain important tools for the CBMC ministry today.

Quotes from Ted DeMoss

"I am firmly convinced that if we can succeed in reaching the business and professional men in our cities for Jesus, we will reach the cities as a whole."

"If businessmen are unchurched, or in church but not 'tuned in,' how are they to be reached for Jesus Christ?"

"Mealtime evangelism will work, but only in direct proportion to our investment in lives through prayer and then time as we bring men out as our guests to well-planned outreach efforts."

"If we are not praying for men by name in our weekly prayer meeting, we should not expect results."

"Only two things in this life have eternal significance: the Word of God and people."

"While the Gospel itself is offensive, you and I should never be offensive."

Ted often spoke about the contrast between one's brief life span on earth and the endless span of eternity. Reflecting on a recent surgery, he said, "You will never know the peace I had as I left my wife and daughters to go into surgery. I told them, 'I'll see you in a few minutes,' knowing whether I lived through the operation or not, I would still be seeing them in a few minutes."

'The Clock of Life'

The clock of life is wound but once,
And no man has the power
To tell just when the hands will stop
At late or early hour.
To lose one's wealth is sad indeed,
To lose one's health is more –
But to lose one's soul is such a loss
That no man can restore.

Slight 'Detour' to the Mayo Clinic

A personal experience epitomized Ted's unusual heart not only for the lost, but also for fellow believers facing difficulty. Although he had retired as CBMC President, Ted maintained an office at the CBMC headquarters. One winter morning I arrived for work and stopped by his office to say hello. "What are you doing today?" he asked. I had planned to do some writing, but no pressing deadlines, so I replied, "I don't have any meetings. What do you have in mind?"

Ted explained he was speaking that day at a CBMC outreach luncheon in Knoxville (about 90 miles away). Donors had continued to fund a plane, a twin-engine Cessna, for his use and he planned to fly it to the event and return soon afterward. He wondered if I wanted to join him, since he would be traveling alone. I agreed to go, expecting to be back in Chattanooga by mid-afternoon.

At the luncheon, Ted spoke as effectively as ever, and a number of guests responded to the invitation to pray with him to ask Jesus Christ into their lives. After he talked briefly with several of them, we went to a local hospital to see Clyde Hawkins, a longtime friend and former National Board member who was dying of a disease called Sjogren's Syndrome.

Then Clyde's wife, Birdie, and his administrative assistant asked for a favor. The Mayo Clinic in Rochester, Minnesota had a possible treatment option for him, but they needed a way to transport him there. Commercial air travel would be impossible for Clyde in his weakened condition. Was there any possibility Ted could fly him there in the CBMC plane – that day?

Ted was very willing. For him, a flight from Knoxville to Minnesota in the small plane wasn't a big deal. The question was, how would I get home? I could rent a car, but Ted asked if I'd like to accompany him, Clyde, Birdie and the assistant. We would still be back home that evening.

I shrugged my shoulders and accepted the invitation to expand our travel itinerary. It was in the days before cellphones, so I used a phone at the hospital to let my wife know that before returning to Chattanooga, we were taking a slight "detour" to Rochester, Minnesota.

After prepping the plane and getting Clyde, his wife and assistant aboard, we headed north, arriving several hours later. Because of the circumstances, the small local airport dispensed with protocol and permitted Ted to taxi the plane into a hanger where an ambulance was already awaiting the patient. Outside, the temperature was below zero and snow covered the ground, so removing Clyde from the aircraft in those conditions was unthinkable.

After everyone else was out of the plane and the ambulance departed for the clinic, Ted taxied back out of the hanger to refuel. He spoke briefly with airport personnel, and we were in the air again bound for Chattanooga, arriving just after nightfall.

Sadly, the treatment plan for Clyde Hawkins at the Mayo Clinic was not successful and he went home to be with his Lord weeks later. But Ted had been obedient to the exhortation of Proverbs 3:27, which says, "Do not withhold good from those to whom it is due, when it in your power to do it." – R.J.T.

Chapter 5 –

'Satisfied Customers'

"And [Jesus] called the twelve and began to send them out two by two...." – Mark 6:7

When considering a major purchase, such as a new car, whose recommendation would you trust the most – a salesperson desperately in need of a commission, or a trusted friend who owns the kind of vehicle you're thinking about buying? Probably the friend, since you would want to know if they're a satisfied customer.

In the 1970s, that became the emphasis of CBMC as it began making a very intentional shift in focus under the leadership of Ted DeMoss and others. After decades of engaging in an assortment of ministries, such as jails, rescue missions, servicemen's centers and open-air evangelistic events, CBMC members began to concentrate on the segment of society they knew best: business and professional men.

As "satisfied customers," they shared a passion for telling others about Jesus Christ and what it meant to follow Him in the everyday world of work. They were like the apostle Paul, who wrote, "Christ's love compels us, because we are convinced that one died for all, and therefore all died" (2 Corinthians 5:14). And who was more equipped than they for reaching out to their peers in the marketplace?

This shift in focus had begun in the early '50s, taking on several facets. One involved refining CBMC's outreach strategy. Mealtime evangelistic meetings – breakfasts, luncheons and sometimes dinners – became an increasingly popular and fruitful way of attracting guests to hear a businessman share his testimony about how he came to know Jesus Christ and what that meant in his life.

Outreach also occurred at special events like weekend retreats, which is where Clay Conner was introduced to the Lord. As recounted in *Men Aflame,* Conner had served as a major in the U.S. Army during World War II, gaining recognition for organizing the Filipino underground in 1943. He had returned from the war bearing scars that were both physical and psychological, having seen many of his fellow soldiers killed or horrifically wounded.

Returning to civilian life, he had started an insurance agency first in New York City and later in Indianapolis, Indiana. One of his first clients was Dr. Robert K. George, a dentist and leader for CBMC in Indianapolis.

George had questioned Conner to determine where he stood spiritually. At one point he inquired, "Clay, have you ever had a real experience with your Creator?" Conner admitted being taken aback by that but, "I expected the nonsense to end." However, his client persisted, even inviting him to a men's retreat in Ohio about a month later.

It's said that persistence neutralizes resistance, and Conner resisted, then reluctantly agreed to attend. That weekend became the turning point of his life.

At the retreat he encountered businessmen much like himself, from Ohio, Michigan and Indiana. Many of these men, actively involved in CBMC groups in their cities, also were different from himself: They carried Bibles, sang hymns together, and prayed.

During the meeting's first early morning prayer session, which Conner was persuaded to attend, still wondering what he was doing there, one man prayed: "Lord, if there is anyone here with us who doesn't know Jesus Christ, may this be his moment of decision. May he give his life over to Thee."

"How does that stranger know about my need?" Conner wondered. "All my life culminated right then and there. The terrible events of the past flashed before me. How thankful I was still to be alive. I prayed silently, 'Lord, if You want my life, take it.'"

The remainder of the retreat turned into an affirmation of his decision to invite Jesus into his life. He returned to Indianapolis a changed man, eagerly reading the Bible every day with a desire for learning more and more about the God he had never known. He soon started a weekly Bible study in his home.

Over time Conner also became active in CBMC, taking on leadership roles, and was able to share his faith with many hundreds of people over the years through his in-house study. This gave him countless opportunities to clearly explain how he had concluded that faith in Jesus Christ was not "nonsense" after all.

Indianapolis became a model city for CBMC, with devoted business and professional men being used by God to touch lives both locally and in other parts of the country. One of them was Jack Brown, an attorney who became one of the ministry's most effective outreach speakers. He utilized his skill to help in equipping more men to give their testimonies in concise, powerful ways at various outreach settings.

CBMC's last open-air outreach meetings had been held in 1976 at the annual convention in Philadelphia, reflecting the changing culture and decreased novelty of such public-speaking events. However, only the venues had changed; the importance of being able to tell one's story of faith never diminished. Nimrod McNair remembered the impact such preparation had not only for himself but also for an "eavesdropper."

As a colonel in the U.S. Air Force, McNair had served as a fighter pilot on 110 combat missions in World War II and Vietnam. After retiring, he became a management consultant promoting ethics based on Judeo-Christian principles.

"One night I went to a function at a Quality Inn. Ted DeMoss, an insurance man from Chattanooga, and Jack Brown, a lawyer from Indianapolis, spoke and helped us learn to give our testimonies. That was my first experience in being taught how to present my relationship with Jesus Christ.

"When the meeting was over," McNair recalled, "we went to retrieve our coats from the young lady at the hotel coat rack. She was crying. When we asked why, she said she had listened to Jack Brown speak from outside the room – this was a men-only event – and she had given her life to Christ!"

This experience and the training had an enduring impact on McNair, who also went on to become a powerful outreach speaker in CBMC for many years. He often would start his talks seeking to connect with the audience by referring to "Monday morning, when the telephone rings and the real world begins again."

Brown's example affected him in another way. McNair also proved very adept in training other outreach speakers for CBMC, not only in his hometown of Atlanta, but also around the country. Prior to his passing in 2017 at the age of 93, McNair had equipped hundreds of speakers to present their testimonies at gatherings sponsored by CBMC and other ministries.

Having speakers well-equipped to tell audiences about how they could experience forgiveness and gain the hope of eternal life through a relationship with Christ, CBMC knew the next challenge was to attract people ready to hear this Good News. The first step in the strategy was to make praying for the unsaved a key part of weekly meetings.

DeMoss introduced a "Ten Most Wanted" card on which men wrote the names of lost business associates, friends, relatives and neighbors. When he was introduced to CBMC, he had seen the power of praying for non-believers by name and thought using this card would serve as a consistent reminder.

Each week, along with Bible study and fellowship, attendees would break into small groups to pray, not only for each other but also for men included on their "Ten Most Wanted" cards. As they saw people on these lists come to faith, it became a cause for rejoicing and encouraged men in CBMC to continue reaching out in the name of Jesus. This also helped to re-energize groups that over time had become too inwardly focused, turning into what could be described as "Coffee Buns More Coffee" gatherings.

A declaration by E.M. Bounds, author of many thought-provoking books on prayer, served as a constant reminder: "How dare we talk to men about God, until we have first talked to God about men?"

Another piece of the evangelistic puzzle was borrowed from a common sales practice. Just as business prospects typically needed to be followed up to close a sale, CBMC leaders recognized a marked card at an outreach meeting was just an initial step toward a genuine, growing relationship with Christ.

Even though he had become one of CBMC's most effective speakers, DeMoss was the first to admit such responses often represented little more than a "cry for help." Experience had taught him that if a message had touched their hearts in some way, outreach guests "would probably pray to the Easter bunny if I told them to," DeMoss often commented.

The Scriptures confirm this in Jesus' parable of the sower (Luke 8:4-18), in which He describes four types of seeds: Seeds that fell along the path, trampled or eaten by birds; seeds falling on rocky ground that withered for lack of moisture; seeds falling among thorns and weeds that quickly choked them off; and seeds that fell on good soil that enabled them to grow and bear much fruit.

Jesus used this metaphor to illustrate what happens in human hearts when the Gospel is presented. Some people never truly listen and respond.

Others respond positively at first, but soon show no evidence of change. Still others seem to receive the Word eagerly, but over time are seduced by worldly concerns. Only the last group become firmly rooted in the truth, begin to grow and eventually start bearing spiritual fruit.

For CBMC, the application of this truth was evident. Many thousands of people had made professions of faith over the years, but there was no way of knowing how they had fared spiritually afterward. Were they flourishing in their faith, bearing fruit for eternity? Were they struggling to understand how to relate their faith to everyday life? Or had they abandoned all pretense of believing and resumed living as if there is no God?

To address this concern, CBMC adopted two distinctive strategies: follow-up, and personal discipleship. (The latter will be addressed in the next chapter.)

Concern for effective follow-up resulted in a unique strategy initially called "Operation Shoeleather" (later renamed Office Visitation). This involved visiting guests in their offices and places of business soon after an outreach event – not only those who had indicated they had prayed to receive Christ, but also guests who had requested more information about what they had heard.

DeMoss and Joe Coggeshall, who joined the CBMC staff full-time about the same time as Ted, had been discussing the need for an effective follow-up program. Coggeshall suggested that Ted go to another city, away from his familiar hometown of Chattanooga, to see if he could devise a way of visiting men effectively.

DeMoss asked him, "Where do you have in mind?" Without hesitation, Coggeshall, a native of the Northeast, replied, "New York City – Manhattan." He felt if a visitation program could work there, it could work anywhere.

"I have to admit, that's about as tough a place as you can go. Millions of men and women travel to New York to work every day, and they don't even live there," DeMoss wrote in his book, *The Gospel and the Briefcase*. "In spite of that, we decided to go. Over the next months I spent several weeks there. The first time I went with one man, and the second time with three others. All day long, from morning until night, we were calling on men in their offices to share Jesus Christ with them – during business hours, no appointments. We never telephoned ahead of time."

After spending a total of about one month in New York, finding considerable success with this innovative approach, DeMoss then went to St. Louis with another man to test the same strategy. "Through hit and miss, trial and error, we developed a program that worked," he said.

One visit in particular validated the importance of such an intentional visitation program. "One fellow told us, 'I've been to three CBMC meetings. I was converted three different times – at three different luncheons.' (At that point, he didn't know the word *saved.*) He said, 'I've always marked on the card that I would like to know more about what's been said. I had never heard from anyone. I decided that you guys didn't mean business, and nine months ago I said I would never go to another meeting. You're the first men from CBMC who have ever showed up here.'"

DeMoss said the philosophy of following up on outreach guests in their workplaces was based on several considerations. "Since a business or professional man spends the majority of his waking hours where he works, we found that was where he was most comfortable being visited. Also, if we attempted to follow up on someone in his home, we had to compete with distractions – his wife, children, the TV set, the dog.

"I remember talking to a very successful businessman in his home, and his wife kept interrupting. She would say things like, 'See, I told you to quit drinking. If you became a Christian, we'd have more money to spend.' He in effect said, 'Shut up!' We obviously weren't winning that man to Christ.

"Eventually we realized the only way we would be able to have a worthwhile visit with a man was to isolate him so he couldn't be distracted by anything. We developed our office visitation program in response to this."

The approach was simple. Visits would be unannounced, not to be rude but to ensure the person being visited would not conjure up an excuse not to talk or start to erect barriers. CBMC representatives would visit by twos, following the biblical pattern Jesus set when He sent out His disciples two-by-two for their first evangelistic visits. This was also practical because one man would talk, while the other could provide silent prayer support. Sometimes the second man would join the conversation if he could relate more directly with something the guest was saying.

Four basic questions would be asked: 1) Did you enjoy the meeting you attended? 2) Was there anything that you did not like about it? 3) What did you think about what the speaker had to say? 4) How did you relate personally to what the speaker said?

"During the course of those questions, we could usually take a man's 'spiritual temperature.' That meant trying to determine whether a man was a Christian, and if he was a non-Christian, how open he was to discussing spiritual matters," DeMoss explained.

His experiences in pioneering office visitation confirmed a belief he had long held, drawn in part from his own spiritual journey. "Anyone who states that business and professional men cannot be reached for Christ just hasn't tried very hard to reach them."

DeMoss recalled an executive he met on an office call. "This businessman was in his sixties. Twice during our conversation, he drove his fist onto his glass-topped desk with such forced that I was afraid the glass would shatter. Both times he said emphatically, 'I need help. Where can I find someone to help me?' He knew he was not a Christian. In fact, he said he had only recently encountered the first Christians he had ever recognized as such – his daughter and son-in-law – who had given their hearts to Jesus Christ in another city and had begun sharing their faith with him.

"After we had spent thirty or forty minutes explaining the Gospel to him, the businessman agreed to become involved in CBMC's four-lesson Bible discussion series, 'First Steps.' Since I was already involved in Bible study and discipleship programs with a number of other people, I paired him up with another CBMC member in our city who started meeting with him faithfully. Three months after that initial visit, I had the privilege of seeing him commit his life to Christ after he had heard me give my testimony at another luncheon."

To expand the use of office visitation across the country, a "blitz" strategy was employed. DeMoss, Coggeshall and other CBMC leaders from across the country would converge on other cities, including Atlanta and Indianapolis. They would call on men who had recently attended outreach in those cities. This approach not only provided manpower for dozens and even hundreds of visits, but also enabled men to learn firsthand how to implement the strategy.

One of those men was Dave Hill, who participated in the "Atlanta blitz" when men made about 300 office calls. Hill, who years later joined the CBMC field staff team, recalled, "Some of the registration cards we used were from years earlier, and it was amazing to find that of all the people who had marked cards (to indicate first-time commitments to Christ), there were zero genuine converts."

Follow-up tools were developed to provide tangible help to guests in understanding the Gospel message. One was *First Steps*, the introductory Bible discussion series DeMoss referred to. It addressed questions such as: Is the Bible credible? Who is Jesus Christ? What was the work of Jesus Christ? How can we be assured of eternal life?

Another tool was *Steps to Peace With God*, which came to be known as "the blue book" because of its blue cover. This little tract, adapted from a booklet created by the Billy Graham Evangelistic Association, communicated four steps for coming to know Christ:

1. God's plan: God loves you and created you to know Him personally.

2. Man's problem: Man is sinful and separated from God, so we cannot know Him personally or experience His love.

3. God's solution: Jesus Christ is God's only provision for man's sin. Through Him we can know God personally and experience God's love.

4. Man's response: We must individually receive Jesus Christ as Savior and Lord; then we can know God personally and experience His love.

This became a standard resource for communicating the Gospel message in a simple, visual way. It was especially useful for guests to have for review at a later time. When people prayed to receive Christ while going through the booklet, their date for making that commitment was often written on the back page.

One other important follow-up tool was *The Reason Why*, a small book by Robert Laidlaw, a New Zealand entrepreneur who built a mail order business into a thriving retail enterprise. He wrote it originally to communicate the story of his personal faith to his staff, which ultimately grew to more than 2,500 people. CBMC used it extensively during the latter half of the 20th century, and many thousands of copies were distributed personally and by mail.

All of these became integral to CBMC's evangelistic strategies and proved very fruitful. Most of them continue to be useful today, including follow-up visitation, the "Ten Most Wanted" card, *Steps to Peace With God*, and *First Steps*.

With a solid outreach philosophy formulated and implemented, the next concern for CBMC, however, was how to ensure "fruit that remains," as described by Jesus in John 15:16. In the next chapter, we'll look at how CBMC addressed that and introduce another key individual in the development and growth of the ministry to business and professional men.

Chapter 6 –

The Importance of Follow-Through

"And the things that you have heard from me in the presence of many witnesses,
entrust to faithful men who will be able to teach others also."
– 2 Timothy 2:2

Picture a labor-and-delivery nurse assisting a young mother giving birth. After the infant makes its appearance, the nurse takes the newborn, performs the standard post-birth evaluation, then wraps it into a tiny blanket. Placing the baby into a crib on wheels, she then pushes it out of the room and down a hallway. She guides the crib and its occupant through the front door of the hospital and into the parking lot. After waving and saying, "Have a good life!" she leaves the infant and reenters the hospital.

Sounds ludicrous, right? Of course. But too often, that's what modern-day evangelism looks like. Someone indicates a profession of faith, people congratulate them and offer words of encouragement, and then leave them as they pursue the next "prospect."

In one sense, the infant in the maternity ward comparison isn't too far-fetched, because the Scriptures make much use of the parenting metaphor to teach principles of spiritual growth. It refers to God as our heavenly Father, of course, and to Jesus as the Son of God. But the analogy doesn't end there.

Writing to believers in the ancient city of Thessalonica, the apostle Paul reminds them, "we were gentle among you, like a mother caring for her little children. We loved you so much that we were delighted to share with you not only the Gospel of God but our lives as well, because you had become so dear to us" (1 Thessalonians 2:7-8).

A few verses later, Paul adds, "For you know that we dealt with each of you as a father deals with his own children, encouraging, comforting and urging you to live lives worthy of God, who calls you into his kingdom and glory" (1 Thessalonians 2:11-12). The apostle also refers to men like Timothy and Silas as his sons in the faith.

The question CBMC had to address beginning in the 1970s was how to relate this parenting concept to the context of the business and professional world. How could it ensure that converts to Christ would become disciples – genuine followers, learners and reproducing representatives of the Lord and His Gospel?

As noted in the last chapter, an introductory Bible study tool called *First Steps* helped in acquainting new believers and seeking non-believers with the basic truths of Bible and Jesus Christ. Ted DeMoss was often amazed at how unaware some people were of facts longtime believers take for granted.

He recalled one couple he was preparing to meet with for the first time. When he called to confirm the meeting, the wife asked what she and her husband should bring. "Well," DeMoss responded, "bring a notepad, a pencil – and a Bible." She replied she did not have a Bible, but added, "I think my husband has one, but it's old. I don't know if it's still good." He assured her that yes, it was still good.

First Steps proved especially useful for instructing about the Bible's credibility and how they could begin an eternal relationship with God through Christ. However, CBMC leaders realized more was needed to help people become established in their faith and embark on a lifelong journey toward spiritual maturity and fruitfulness.

This was where Joe Coggeshall and others assumed pivotal roles. Coggeshall, a native of Cape Cod, Massachusetts, at one time envisioned a career in major league baseball as a pitcher. An outstanding athlete, he had signed with the Boston Red Sox and was showing promise in the team's minor league system when he suffered a career-ending injury to his throwing arm.

With the sport quickly fading in his rearview mirror, Coggeshall enlisted in the U.S. Navy and was assigned to a ship in the Mediterranean Sea, off the coast of Italy. While on shore leave, Coggeshall would go to a Naval recreation center in Naples managed by Pete George, who was associated with The Navigators. During those visits, the two began talking about the Bible and Jesus Christ. During those interactions, Coggeshall committed his life to the Lord, although it took his wife, Gladys, a few more years to give her heart to Christ.

George stayed close to them both and began helping Joe grow in his faith using study materials developed by The Navigators, which included a very intentional Scripture memory program. After Gladys came to know Christ, they both began flourishing in their faith and caught a vision for sharing the Gospel and helping others to become true followers of Jesus.

Following his stint in the Navy, Coggeshall joined George in working with The Navigators and became adept at using their discipling materials. Later he, and then George, became involved with CBMC and joined its full-time staff. For a time, Coggeshall served as a field staff director traveling across the entire country.

Both drew from their Navigator experience to instill vision and passion for discipling into the CBMC ministry. What Ted DeMoss had done for personal evangelism, Coggeshall did as a champion for one-on-one discipling.

Until he arrived, CBMC had no formalized discipleship strategy. Starting with materials originated by the Navs, he and George set about developing a discipling prototype tailored for CBMC's unique audience. They drew from the "Design for Discipleship" studies and began writing new content that would be called "*Operation Timothy*."

The title was taken from 2 Timothy 2:2, in which the apostle Paul, writing to his protégé, Timothy, exhorted, "And the things you have heard from me in the presence of many witnesses, entrust to faithful men who will be able to teach others also." This single verse served as a model of spiritual reproduction, showing four generations of believers – Paul, Timothy, "faithful men" and "others."

Duane Jacobs, a CBMC leader in Fort Wayne, Indiana before serving as CBMC's Director of Administration in Chattanooga from 1980 to 1983, recalled being among those who field-tested the new materials.

"Joe and Pete came into Fort Wayne with the first drafts of *Operation Timothy* and tried it with the three committees there to get feedback. They both were familiar with the Navigators' materials and methodology, and worked at writing introductory materials and then more advanced studies for CBMC."

Scripture memory became an integral part of the discipling strategy, and George served as a role model. He demonstrated a great command of the Scriptures, having memorized hundreds of passages, meditating on them, living it out and teaching others how to put them into practice.

Coggeshall also became a local leader for CBMC in Atlanta, where he had relocated, and God used him to have a lasting impact in the lives of many men and couples there. One of them was Dave Rathkamp, who was head tennis professional at Cherokee Town & Country Club when he committed his life to Christ.

Rathkamp, a native of Rhode Island and a fellow New Englander, recalled, "I had been invited to a CBMC conference in South Carolina in 1976, shortly after I was converted, and there I met Joe. After we came back to Atlanta, he called me and in late 1976 or early 1977, we started meeting in *Operation Timothy.*

"Joe started taking tennis lessons from me, and later his wife, Gladys, took lessons as well. He would buy things from me in our pro shop at the country club, which I liked, and our relationship started growing from there."

Rathkamp described Coggeshall as "a tremendously faithful guy. He was very persistent in meeting with men, and always followed through on his commitments. He lived according to Luke 16:10, in which Jesus said, 'he who is faithful in little things also will be faithful in much.'

"But Joe would not just meet with any man. He met with men he felt had huge potential for the Gospel. He referred to FAT men – Faithful, Available, and Teachable. And when he spoke, his messages were always based on the Word, teaching from what he had hidden in his heart, as Psalm 119:11 teaches. Many men's lives were greatly changed through Joe's ministry of discipling and disciplemaking."

Coggeshall became known for his direct, even blunt style of communicating, but Rathkamp said that contributed to his effectiveness in ministering to others. "Joe was very forceful. Either you loved him or you hated him – but most people loved him. With him there was only one way, and he would let you know what it was. He was deeply committed to the Lord Jesus.

"Early on I started listening closely to what Joe said to do. I remember him talking about memorizing Bible verses. I told him I couldn't memorize. He said, 'Oh, that's okay. What's your street address?' I told him. Then he asked, 'What's your phone number?' After I told him that, Joe replied, 'That's pretty good. Now I think you can start learning some verses.'

"Not long afterward, we were meeting and he asked if I'd learned my memory verse for the week. I said no, I hadn't. Joe simply said, 'That's okay. Let's learn it right now,' and he started working with me to learn the assigned verse there in the restaurant.

"That verse was 1 John 5:11-12, 'And this is the testimony: that God has given us eternal life, and this life is in His Son. He who has the Son has life; he who does not have the Son of God does not have life.' After we worked on learning this verse, Joe said, 'Dave, when you go out into the world you run into all kinds of people. But there are really only two kinds of people in the world: those who have eternal life, and those who don't have eternal life.' I never forgot that.

"Joe ingrained the basics of the Christian life into me. He also became involved with my family, and he and Gladys had a great impact on me, my wife, Donna, and our children. He was a gregarious, fun-loving guy, but most of all he loved the Lord."

Rathkamp noted Coggeshall and DeMoss balanced each other with their approaches to ministry. "He and Ted had great respect for each other. One was an evangelist, the other was a disciplemaker. They had a lot of battles over ministry philosophy and strategy over the years, but always had a lot of mutual appreciation. Joe had a lot of influence on Ted, giving him the vision for using a tool like *First Steps* materials with non-believers and brand-new believers."

Another man that knew Coggeshall very well was Dave Hill, who had come to faith through CBMC and eventually served in several staff roles, including Atlanta Metro Director and Southeastern Division Director. Larry Parker, who regularly participated in a variety of CBMC activities, was Hill's spiritual father.

At Parker's invitation, Hill attended a CBMC meeting at a downtown Atlanta hotel in 1972. After the meeting, Parker and Coggeshall visited his office to get his feedback. Hill candidly told them it was not the kind of meeting he desired to attend again, since it felt to him like a church service, with singing and praying out loud, "very religious." The hotel was also located in a part of the city where Hill, who was in the insurance business at the time, did not feel comfortable.

As a result, with Coggeshall and Parker, Hill helped to form a new CBMC in downtown Atlanta, separating completely from the group that originally had been chartered in 1938. This gave Hill countless opportunities to observe Coggeshall in action.

When the Rev. Billy Graham came to Atlanta for a crusade in 1975,

Coggeshall was involved with some of the organizing and follow-up work. After the crusade, he and his wife, Gladys, hosted a dinner in their home where he gave his testimony and announced a men's Bible study that would start the following Sunday night, focusing on basic Bible doctrine.

Attendees at that study included Hill and Parker, Deane Stokes, Bill Shaw, Dr. Bob Nelson, Clarence Neal and John McKinley, all of whom became key figures in the work of CBMC in Atlanta.

Coggeshall continually emphasized Matthew 28:19-20 and the Great Commission, reminding them of Jesus' charge to "go and make disciples" at many of the meetings. He also used Isaiah 60:22 – "one shall become a thousand" – as a source of inspiration and challenge.

"He often talked about having a vision for 100 years out from your life, seeing multiple generations of believers going forward. Spiritual multiplication was his passion," Hill said. "I might have been one of the first people taken through the true *Operation Timothy*. At that time, the pages were duplicated on a mimeograph machine."

Describing the man whom many considered "larger than life," Hill observed, "I used to call him a bull in a china cabinet. His was a voice that wanted to be heard, and he was certainly anointed by the Lord. He could be overpowering, especially in meetings, but his heart was always in the right place – eager to tell others about Christ and help believers grow in their faith through *Operation Timothy*.

"His wife, Gladys, kept him in tow. She was very hospitable; they had people in their home all the time. Together they ministered to couples well, but Joe was much more effective with men than with couples – he was a little brash and could sometimes offend.

"Joe was in my face like crazy, telling me I needed to get involved in discipling someone. Then I got connected with Bruce Witt and his wife, Dana, and later Dave Rathkamp."

Witt, who became another in the long line of people God reached out to through Coggeshall, echoed personal observations about him. "Joe was a big teddy bear with a real soft heart. He was very engaging; a great storyteller. He loved to evangelize and disciple. Joe had a passion for the world.

"He was forthright and tenacious; he was as strong as he could be in challenging people involved in evangelism and discipleship. He helped us understand that discipling is life-on-life, not just a Bible study."

At one CBMC conference, Coggeshall joined a number of other men to show what a "discipling tree" looked like. They included George Sanchez, who had been discipled by Dawson Trotman, the late founder of The Navigators. Sanchez had proceeded to disciple Pete George. Sanchez and George were joined by Coggeshall, John Shoop, Clif Campbell, Rathkamp, Hill and Witt, all of whom had gone through *Operation Timothy* and were actively discipling others. It was an amazing example of spiritual multiplication.

In addition to *Operation Timothy,* another of Coggeshall's contributions to the CBMC ministry toolbox was in helping to develop resources for lifestyle evangelism and discipling. First, he had a role in producing the *Lifestyle Evangelism Seminar (LES),* which consisted of a series of brief videos with a companion discussion guide.

Then in the mid-1980s, working with Jim Petersen of The Navigators and consultant Pat MacMillan, they developed a more polished *"Living Proof: Evangelism"* film and training series, drawing from Petersen's books, *Evangelism as a Lifestyle* and *Living Proof.* Together they wrote the script, and then oversaw filming and production.

Coggeshall had developed a network of LES trainers, including Fritz Klumpp, a pilot for Delta Airlines who later became Executive Director of CBMC. The *Living Proof* video series, featuring a more dramatic story line, made it easier to train people in principles of lifestyle/relational evangelism.

In the early 1990s a sequel, *Living Proof: Discipleship*, was developed and produced. This time Coggeshall worked with David Stoddard, Witt, Petersen and other Navigator staff members to use the format to teach the philosophy and principles of one-on-one discipling and disciple-making.

It was produced first for CBMC, but then Stoddard and Witt led an effort to take the training to churches, equipping pastors to teach the principles to their leaders and congregations.

Through the years each of these resources have undergone revision, both in design and content, to reflect the changing business environment without compromising underlying biblical truths about evangelism and discipling.

The original *Operation Timothy* materials, which had plain orange, yellow and red covers, were updated in 1995 into a series now known as *Operation Timothy Classic.* Another updated and redesigned edition, *Operation Timothy Signature,* was introduced in 2008, and the two most recent editions became available through Amazon.com in 2001. Both of the newer versions were made available digitally in 2014 on CBMC's website.

Operation Timothy also has been translated into more than a dozen different languages through CBMC International.

In addition, the lifestyle evangelism training has been further refined into *LivingProof Adventure,* a video-based series for small groups. Over 13 sessions, the series presents 12 principles that undergird the understanding of evangelism as a lifestyle, not an event. It is proving very effective as a starting tool for new CBMC cities and teams.

Coggeshall passed away in February 26, 2009, leaving a rich legacy that CBMC has continued to build on ever since.

Chapter 7

Evangelism: A Process, Not an Event

*"But in your hearts set apart Christ as Lord. Always be prepared
to give an answer to everyone who asks you to give the reason for the hope
that you have. But do this with gentleness and respect." – 1 Peter 3:15*

The 1980s ushered in an era of American society very different from the earlier decades in which CBMC had ministered. It was marked by a decided shift toward "secular humanism." Christian scholars began discussing and writing about "post-modernism," describing the United States as a "post-Christian" society. Almost imperceptibly, the established Judeo-Christian culture had started losing traction.

As a consequence, bumper stickers of the '70s that had proclaimed, "Christ is the Answer," often prompted the reaction, "But what is the question?" Direct, confrontational evangelistic methods encountered more resistance and less success.

God was not surprised. He began awakening many within the Christian community to a need for redirecting evangelistic approaches toward "relational evangelism." As society drifted away from a commonly accepted consensus on matters of faith, the importance of earning the right to be heard was gaining acceptance.

Almost simultaneously, three pivotal books were published by authors on the same topic, but from somewhat different perspectives. They were *Lifestyle Evangelism* by Joe Aldrich, a pastor; *Out of the Saltshaker and into the World* by Rebecca Manley Pippert, who had served on the staff of InterVarsity Christian Fellowship; and *Evangelism as a Lifestyle* by Jim Petersen, a longtime staff member with The Navigators.

Drawing from their distinctive experiences, all shared a common understanding: contemporary evangelism was most effective within the context of growing, caring relationships. Aldrich wrote: "You have to be good news before you can share Good News," and "People want to know how much you care before they care how much you know."

This reality wasn't lost on the leadership of CBMC. More and more people in the marketplace were coming from secularized, unchurched backgrounds, meaning they had little or no basic familiarity with or understanding of the Bible, its truths and precepts. The "starting line" in evangelism had moved.

In response, CBMC began to develop training tools to impart the principles of lifestyle evangelism, teaching how to build relationships with people who weren't losing sleep over how to get their lives right with God. The first step was to create the *Lifestyle Evangelism Seminar,* a series of dramatic video training sessions with accompanying workbooks that could be used at weekly prayer meetings, as well as in-home Bible studies.

Joe Coggeshall was a central figure in development of this resource in 1982. Using professional actors, directors and producers, the series focused on two businessmen, one being a Christian and the other an unchurched non-believer.

Over the course of the presentation, the drama segments depicted a growing friendship between the two, ultimately resulting in the previously resistant agnostic coming to know Jesus Christ in an unforgettable way.

Originally called the Personal Development Seminar, more than 2,000 people were trained during LES weekends led by Coggeshall, along with weekly CBMC prayer meetings.

Building on this initial foray into the Hollywood-style film medium, in 1990 CBMC partnered with author Petersen for a video adaptation of his follow-up book, *Living Proof: Sharing the Gospel Naturally.* Coggeshall and another member of the CBMC executive staff team, David Stoddard, collaborated on this project, called *Living Proof: Evangelism.*

Designed for use in homes with couples as well as men's groups, the series depicted a well-intended Christian businessman using – and misusing – principles of lifestyle evangelism. The visual impact of the videos helped participants gain an understanding that evangelism, especially in an increasingly secularized society and sometimes antagonistic business environment, must be approached primarily as "a process, and not an event."

Rather than a one-size-fits-all approach that some evangelistic programs insisted on, the *Living Proof* approach followed biblical exhortations such as, "Conduct yourselves with wisdom toward outsiders, making the most of every opportunity; let your speech be with grace, seasoned as it were with salt, so you will know how to respond to each person" (Colossians 4:5-6).

Another passage, 1 Peter 3:15, undergirded this approach of seeking to interact graciously and with sensitivity with those outside of the family of faith: "But in your hearts set apart Christ as Lord. Always be prepared to give an answer to everyone who asks you to give the reason for the hope that you have. But do this with gentleness and respect."

The principle behind this was that if we're giving an answer, or as another translation states it, "make a defense," that implies the other person has raised a question or has presented an opportunity to defend what we believe.

To address the discipleship portion of CBMC's twofold purpose, a second video series, *Living Proof: Discipleship,* was produced in 1995 under the guidance of Stoddard and Coggeshall, based on another book Petersen had written about discipling others.

Both series not only taught how to effectively build redemptive relationships with non-believers, but also how to live out one's faith with integrity in ways that reflect the transforming power of Jesus Christ.

With CBMC always striving to find innovative ways for presenting these timeless truths and principles, Mike Marker of Cincinnati, Ohio in 2000 developed *Straight to the Source.* It was another training video with discussion guide that taught how to lead a group through an open-ended discussion of the Gospel of John.

Featuring Marker, who had led discussions like this numerous times, and Petersen, this movie-style video dramatized two sessions of the seeker-friendly discussion formats.

"The series was based on a series of what we called 'John studies' we initiated in Cincinnati in 1993," he said. "The first one I did with my wife, Carol, one of our daughters and her fiancé, and a couple Carol had met. The woman was a Jewish believer, but her husband was not. We spent two weeks talking about the first chapter of the Gospel of John, and then each week we covered another chapter.

"The Gospel uses the word 'believe' more than 90 times, and it's impossible to miss what God is asking us to do. After we had gone through the third or fourth chapter, the husband walked in one evening and declared, 'I did it!', meaning he had prayed to give his life to Christ. He had decided to believe on the Lord Jesus and be saved.

"He very soon put his faith into action by telling his mother, who also was Jewish, that he had trusted in Jesus. He picked her up at the airport when she arrived for a visit, and couldn't even wait until they got home. My friend (Harold), was carrying out the admonition of Romans 10:9, 'That if you confess with your mouth, "Jesus is Lord," and believe in your heart that God raised him from the dead, you will be saved.'"

Marker said the approach of the John studies was "so simple; it's not higher math. We started by using questions Jim Petersen printed in the back of his book, *Living Proof,* to launch discussion. Such as, based on what we have read in the chapter, 'Who is Jesus?' and 'What does He expect of me?' Then, based on how they answer, we ask another question.

"We don't have to be the expert. We have no religious talk about church. We don't teach or preach; we let the Holy Spirit do that. We just keep bringing the discussion back to Jesus. And we don't have a harvesting mentality. We just let the Spirit move in His time, letting the Word of God do its work."

The use of the Gospel of John studies, along with application of *Living Proof* principles, has continued to grow in Cincinnati. Marker says at any time there are about six of those studies going on in the area. "Almost all of our leaders met Christ through the John study. It's become part of our DNA, and it's become a feeder for our whole ministry."

Marker, a homebuilder at the time, was already a young believer when he was introduced to CBMC in 1981. He was trying to understand what it meant to be a Christian and had started attending a Bible study at the offices of a law firm in downtown Cincinnati.

"But after about six months, I was kind of tired of trying, so I went up to a guy at church and said I needed some help. He said he knew of another guy in the church who met with young guys, and that's when I met John Bird, who was involved with CBMC. He told me about something called *Operation Timothy,* and we started meeting once a week. Then his wife, Carole, began meeting with my wife and we also spent time together as couples.

"About six months later, I asked John how long we were going to continue meeting, and he replied, 'Until you get a Timothy of your own.' The next week I started to meet with another guy, an attorney."

As the years passed, Marker took on leadership roles with CBMC locally and then as a member of the National Board. While CBMC's Southeastern Family Conference was being held in Lookout Mountain, Georgia, he and his family attended initially as guests of the Birds and then went for a number of years on their own. There he met men like Joe Coggeshall, Houston Metro Director Dave Rathkamp, Atlanta Metro Director Dave Hill and others, all of whom helped him not only to refine his ministry skills but also to gain a clearer vision for how he could serve the Lord in the marketplace.

"About five years ago I started praying fervently for the next generation of CBMC leaders in Cincinnati. We've been here now for about 40 years, and I'm looking forward to what God is going to do in the years to come."

In keeping with the principle of building relationships with the hope of earning the right to be heard, CBMC groups around the country also developed a variety of alternatives to traditional mealtime outreach meetings. These included golf and tennis tournaments, fishing trips, snow skiing, group excursions to professional baseball and football games, rodeos, and job-hunting and networking workshops.

Annual community prayer breakfasts, often in collaboration with local mayors and county officials and coordinated by CBMC groups, had been in existence since the 1960s. They proliferated across the United States in the '80s and '90s as another way for attracting non-Christians to a non-threatening event where hundreds, and sometimes thousands, of business and professional people, civic leaders and law enforcement officers would be in attendance.

Notable people from the surrounding community would offer welcomes and prayers before a main speaker, typically someone of national prominence and credibility, would speak. They would speak about their personal lives and career experiences, but also interweave the Gospel message, before closing by offering a prayer with an invitation for attendees to pray to receive Jesus Christ as Savior and Lord.

Through the years, the "lifestyle evangelism" approach, coupled with CBMC's arsenal of ministry tools and events, has proved extremely fruitful in helping business and professional men to discover their need for forgiveness, redemption and restoration that only God can provide. As the apostle Paul wrote, "We loved you so much that we were delighted to share with you not only the Gospel of God but our lives as well, because you had become so dear to us" (1 Thessalonians 2:8).

Chapter 8

Advancing into the Urban Marketplaces

"And you will be My witnesses, in Jerusalem, and in all
Judea and Samaria…." – Acts 1:8

At the onset of the 1980s, CBMC embarked on a new initiative designed to expand its impact into more metropolitan areas across the United States. Under the title of Metro 80:80, the goal for this program was to establish a fruitful CBMC presence in each of the 80 largest U.S. cities during the '80s.

Albert Page, a retired IBM executive who had been actively involved with CBMC in several cities and served as a member of the National Board, was hired as Director of Metro Development to spearhead this emphasis. Target cities were identified according to census demographics, which showed that approximately seven percent of metro populations consisted of business and professional men.

To help in launching new or greater ministry in these areas, foundation grants had been obtained, providing seed money for temporarily funding Metro Directors for cities where little or no ministry existed. In some cases, CBMC ministries in established cities helped to support staff men, sending them as missionaries to other metro areas.

Prior to 1980, only a handful of staff men were working full-time to oversee ministries locally and regionally. These included Max Webb of Overland Park, Kansas; Jim Brady of Sacramento, California; Ed Seale of Vienna, Virginia; Dave Hill of Atlanta, Georgia; Ken Johnson of St. Paul, Minnesota; Ralph Spencer of Fort Myers, Florida, and Clif Campbell of Winter Park, Florida.

The underlying concept of Metro 80:80 was that volunteer leaders, with family, work and other obligations, were limited in how much time and energy they could give to growing the work of CBMC in their cities. Men like Ted DeMoss, Joe Coggeshall, Webb, Brady and Roy LeTourneau were traveling around the country to speak at CBMC events and interact with local committees, but having full-time staff in place would enhance the growth and depth of local ministries.

The first Metro Director hired was Dave Rathkamp, a former tennis teaching professional who had come to know Jesus Christ through the CBMC ministry in Atlanta, and was discipled by Joe Coggeshall, Dave Hill and others. In 1981, he was assigned to Houston, Texas, where one CBMC group had been meeting.

Rathkamp, with the help and encouragement of his wife, Donna, immediately came alongside existing leaders and set about discipling men one-on-one, casting a new vision for reaching the city's marketplace for Christ, and sharpening the focus of prayer breakfasts, outreach meetings and other events.

Over the next several years the work of CBMC began growing in Metro Houston in a variety of ways, both in depth and breadth. Along with regular evangelistic outreach events, *Operation Timothy* became an integral resource for helping men become established in their faith. The fruit of those early days is continuing to be harvested today.

In 1981, two other Metro Directors were appointed: Larry Kendrick, who had been on the CBMC administrative staff since 1977, was sent to Metro Philadelphia, where he worked with a core of CBMC veterans to build the ministry within the city and its suburbs. Arnie Bandstra, an engineer in Wheaton, Illinois, who had come to know Christ through CBMC, became the first Metro Director in Chicago.

Then in 1983, Ken Johnson was hired as Director of Field Operations and moved with his family from suburban St. Paul to Chattanooga to oversee the recruitment of new staff directors.

When he had originally come on staff with CBMC in 1978, there were two CBMC committees, one in Minneapolis and one in St. Paul. Working with volunteer leaders like Chuck Eumurian, Dick Nelson and Dale Madison, Johnson had seen that number grow to 17 CBMC groups in the Twin Cities before he assumed his new national responsibilities.

Between 1983 and 1991, he was directly involved with the screening, evaluating and hiring of 31 Metro Directors. In some instances, as ministry grew in some cities, more than one staff director was added when financial support became available. Other Metro areas where field staff men were sent during the 1980s included:

Seattle; Fresno, California; Baltimore; Rapid City, South Dakota; Miami; St. Louis; Oklahoma City; Detroit; Omaha, Nebraska; Salt Lake City;

Ft. Wayne, Indiana; Chattanooga; New York City/New Jersey; Denver; Minneapolis/St. Paul; Kansas City; Phoenix; New Orleans; Columbus, Ohio; Orange County, California; Mobile, Alabama; Portland, Oregon; Pittsburgh, Pennsylvania, and Anchorage, Alaska.

Fred Zillich, who became Detroit's first Metro Director in 1984 and then succeeded Johnson as Field Staff Director in 1991, discovered the impact a full-time staff person could have on a local ministry.

"The same as having a church without a pastor, in many cases a local CBMC ministry can only go so far. Volunteer leaders can do very well, but they have their own full-time jobs and responsibilities. We often found that full-time staff were better prepared for training and equipping men in the local ministry, and encouraging them to become more deeply involved.

"Before I came on staff, no one in Detroit had ever been to Chattanooga for training. Through the training I received, as a local team we were able to gain a vision for the ministry we never had before. All of the major automotive companies had places where CBMC groups could meet on-site, like the GM Tech Center.

"These were places we never would have gotten into without a vision for the city. After we were able to establish a ministry presence there, more of our guys started attending National Conventions and conferences, being exposed to ministry tools, how they were used, and gaining a world vision. Workshops, training sessions and solid Bible teaching there all had a strong impact on our ministry in Metro Detroit."

The Metro 80:80 program didn't fully succeed in its stated goal of establishing CBMC ministries in the 80 largest U.S. cities during the decade. In some cases, placing a staff man in a city did not result in rousing success. However, in many areas the ministry did take root or became more fruitful than it had been, and countless lives were changed partly because a Metro Director had helped to launch a new work in a city.

One example was in New York City, where Bob Wishon had moved from St. Louis to work at building the ministry as Metro Director. One of his first CBMC leaders was Dick Arthur, president of a financial firm on Wall Street who was a key to starting a group in Lower Manhattan. Among the beneficiaries were Jerry Molnar and his wife, Camy, a couple who lived across the Hudson River in Bayonne, New Jersey.

The Molnars traveled daily by car or train into the city where they both worked. Jerry was operations manager for a brokerage firm, later becoming a "headhunter" for the securities industry; Camy became Arthur's administrative assistant. Before that, however, they had to begin their spiritual journey which brought them out of a life of alcoholism and substance abuse.

They had met at a nightclub where she was a dancer. When Camy won first runner-up in a Miss New Jersey beauty pageant, Jerry said, "I figured I better get moving before she found somebody else." After getting married, they both came to faith while attending support group meetings for victims of chemical abuse. They joined a local church and began to grow spiritually.

In 1986, Jerry attended his first CBMC luncheon on 42nd Street in Manhattan. "My pastor's wife had heard about CBMC, and she thought I might be interested. So, I went to a luncheon, there were about 100 men in attendance, and I loved the meeting," he said.

There he met Arthur for the first time. He invited Jerry to a different CBMC gathering the following week and they soon started going through *Operation Timothy* together.

"At first my idea was that I could meet a lot of Christians through CBMC to do business with and make a lot of money. But after Dick and Bob Wishon came to visit me in my office and explained what CBMC is really all about, I was hooked."

After learning the value of being discipled through *Operation Timothy,* Jerry began discipling other men, became chairman of the CBMC group on Wall Street, and led Bible studies in the North Tower of the World Trade Center, where he had an office on the 79th floor until 2001. He and Camy also began conducting a Bible study for recovering addicts in their home.

God's providential care and Jerry's presence at the World Trade Center twice intersected in dramatic ways. On Feb. 26, 1993, a 1,200-pound bomb was detonated inside a rental truck that was parked in a public parking garage below the Trade Center. The intent was to send the North Tower crashing into the South Tower, bringing both down and killing many thousands of people inside the buildings.

Although the terrorist attack failed in that goal, six people were killed and more than 1,000 were injured. The site was the garage where the Molnars typically parked their car when they drove to work. However, that morning

Camy had been ill and Jerry chose to stay home with her. If not for her being sick, they likely would have been on the scene at the time of the bombing.

The second event was the terrorist attack on the Trade Center's twin towers on September 11, 2001, which took the lives of nearly 3,000 people. Once again Jerry's life was spared with Camy providing the reason, except this time in a very indirect way.

About two months earlier, the couple had attended a CBMC World Convention in Atlanta. She had not been feeling well when they arrived, and when her discomfort increased, they went to a local hospital where they consulted with medical staff. Her symptoms were misdiagnosed as kidney stones. Days later, while still in Atlanta, she died of an aneurysm in her abdominal aorta. Hundreds attended her memorial service, including CBMC friends from around the country.

This ironically set the stage for Jerry not being in the World Trade Center when the two commandeered jets were flown directly into the towers, resulting in their total destruction.

He had moved his office to 30 Broad Street, about two blocks from the New York Stock Exchange. But since he still received mail at his old address, Jerry's routine was to ride the subway into the concourse below the World Trade Center, take the elevator up to the 79th floor of the North Tower, check on his mail and spend some time visiting with friends. Then he would descend the tower and walk down Broadway to his new office.

That morning, however, he uncharacteristically overslept. A native New Yorker and lifelong fan of the New York Giants, the night before he had stayed up to watch the Giants on "Monday Night Football," not getting to bed until after midnight.

"The high-tech alarm clock-CD player my daughter, Rene, had bought for Camy as a Christmas gift the year before didn't go off. One of the things I didn't learn how to do properly was set the alarm, so it didn't awaken me when I had planned," Jerry said. "By the time I woke up, my schedule was already shot to pieces. I knew I would never be able to make my first two appointments that morning.

"So I did something else that was out of character for me: Instead of rushing around like the crazed, time-dominated city guy that I am, I casually brewed a pot of coffee, got the morning newspaper off the porch, and sat down to catch up on the previous day's news as I consumed several cups of coffee. 'What am I doing?' I thought to myself once or twice, but I just kept reading the paper."

It was only when the phone rang and heard his other daughter, Robin, describe the horrific events that had unfolded that morning just 10 miles away that Jerry learned how providentially he had avoided becoming one of the casualties. Robin had called, frantically wanting to know where he was and if he was all right.

"I quickly turned on the small TV set that Camy had put in our kitchen and sat transfixed, in stunned silence – again, out of character for me – and tried to comprehend what was happening to the towers and the people inside that had been such a big part of my life for many years."

He recalled a Bible study he had attended on the North Tower's 79th floor just one week before with four young men, along with three older men. The topic had been about being prepared for the end of one's life. "The younger guys all said, 'We're ready to go,' while the older guys – all grandfathers – admitted they weren't so ready. The North Tower was the first to get hit, and all four of the younger men died when it came down. The older men weren't there when it happened."

Jerry knew many other men and women who perished in the terrorist attack. Incredibly, because Camy had not been there to make sure his alarm clock had been set properly, he was not among them.

But CBMC played yet another role in turning his sad story into a happy one. About two years later, he was speaking at a CBMC International conference in Mexico where he met a widow named Gracie. Her late husband had been active in CPEC, the Latin American equivalent of CBMC. She and Jerry struck up a friendship, they began a courtship and got married in 2004. They now live in Round Rock, Texas, a suburb of Austin.

Not every story is as dramatic as is Jerry Molnar's, but as CBMC has maintained its resolve to advance into cities and metropolitan areas across the United States, thousands of men, their wives and families, coworkers and companies have been touched by God for eternity.

Chapter 9 –

Like Father, Like Son

"And these words which I command you today shall be in your heart. You shall teach them diligently to your children…when you sit in your home, when you walk by the way, when you lie down, and when you rise up."
– Deuteronomy 6:6-7

Throughout CBMC's history, one of the exciting developments has been the passing of the ministry's vision from one generation to the next. Especially when it's from father to son. One of the first illustrations of this was R.G. LeTourneau, the legendary industrialist who became a key figure in the work of CBMC in its early years, and his son, Roy LeTourneau, who provided influential CBMC leadership both in the United States and internationally.

We could cite many other outstanding examples of father-son teams in CBMC through the years, but for purposes of illustration, let's consider Ron Bundy, who went home to be with his Lord in 2018, and his son, Mark. Both have played major roles for the CBMC ministry in Southern California, where they built careers and established their families, and have had meaningful impact in other parts of the country.

Ron spent more than 50 years of his life in civil engineering, including a three-year tour with the Navy Civil Engineer Corps (Seabees) while stationed in the Great Lakes area. His specialty was the design and construction of dams, sewage and drainage projects.

Since he had majored in engineering at UCLA, after being discharged from the Navy he and his wife, Marlene, returned to Southern California. They eventually settled in the city of Irvine, in Orange County.

Having been raised by missionary parents ministering in Guatemala, Ron decided to attend Fuller Seminary in Pasadena while he was working part-time with an engineering company. This led to his first encounter with CBMC – and a new perspective on ministry.

"I was introduced to CBMC in Pasadena, where there was a pretty active group. I've been involved with CBMC ever since, except for times when we were in South America and Sri Lanka on business. Even then I was meeting with men either one-on-one or in small groups, seeking to help them grow in their faith," he explained during an interview.

Through CBMC, Ron met dedicated Christian businessmen like Lorin Griset, an insurance executive who also served many years as mayor of Santa Ana and founded CBMC in that city. These men helped him understand he didn't have to become a missionary or pastor to serve God full-time.

"Knowing my family background, and that I had several sisters also involved in mission work, people often would ask me, 'Why aren't you a missionary?' But I've always believed that as an engineer, I am one. Serving the Lord through my work – and CBMC – has really been my ministry. We're God's ambassadors in the places where we work. That's our mission field, serving the Lord and others right where we are."

Ron's son, Mark, along with their other children, Timothy and Lisa, were exposed to the CBMC ministry early on. Mark in particular captured Ron's enthusiasm for being able to serve God and others through the workplace.

"I came to know the Lord at age 6," he said, "and my dad has been a great example for me. I've watched him mentor guys for more than 50 years. He was one of the early proponents of CBMC in our area."

Mark became involved in the work of CBMC in his mid- to late-20s, and has been attending weekly breakfast groups in Santa Ana and speaking at events ever since. "It's been a great benefit being able to partner with my father in this ministry. He's an engineer, and I'm more of a sales guy, so we're wired very differently, but have been able to work together well."

Working in general construction for more than 35 years on commercial, retail and industrial projects, Mark has had many opportunities to use CBMC as a platform for sharing his faith and investing in the lives of men, using *Operation Timothy* as he had seen his father do so many times.

"Some years ago, one of my Timothys was on the verge of divorce. He was in *Operation Timothy* with me, and we had developed a strong Paul/Timothy relationship. God spoke to him during the weeks we were meeting together, and eventually he flipped the whole relationship with his wife. Now they are doing very well in their marriage. That's a strong indicator that what we are doing is working."

A resident of Costa Mesa, Mark has enjoyed the practicality of CBMC, spending "so many years working with men and seeing their lives changed. It's helped to strengthen my own faith, becoming the man of God that He intended for me to be, as husband to Leslie and father of two sons. I've had opportunities to teach, lead and facilitate CBMC groups – it's given me a track to run on, as well as my involvement with my church.

"What's great about CBMC is coming alongside and supporting men in their own personal ministry to others, going to multiple generations. It's not just a one and done kind of thing. And it complements our work in the business world, affirming that our business is our ministry, showing us how to integrate our faith 24/7 into the workday. Business owners, CEOs, managers – it gives them a built-in platform for inviting people to hear a testimony of how Jesus has changed a man's life."

Almost until the day he died, Ron faithfully attended CBMC prayer meetings twice a week – on Tuesdays in Santa Ana (where the CBMC office is located), and Newport Beach. Ron was a leader in the Newport Beach CBMC for many years, and was succeeded in that role by Mark. His other son, Timothy, has also been involved with CBMC.

"It's been an unbelievable experience for me, seeing Mark go on – and pass me – in many respects." Ron said.

He recalled walking past a meeting room a few years ago and hearing his last name, Bundy, mentioned. "I poked my head in and asked, 'Was someone talking about me?' The response, with a laugh, was, 'We're not talking about you. We want Mark. We want the young guy.' Hearing that didn't bother me a bit. In fact, I felt really good about it.

"It's been marvelous to see Mark become so involved with CBMC, especially with his personality. If my own involvement in CBMC had resulted in nothing more than encouraging and challenging Mark, it would have all been worth it," Ron stated

"Everybody wants Mark on their team. He's always got time for ministry, locally and nationally. Mark had been to a lot of CBMC meetings with me, but it was at a President's Council weekend in Northern California years ago that Mark really became interested in getting more deeply involved."

Mark vividly recalled that weekend as well. "Fritz Klumpp (who was serving as CBMC's Executive Director at the time) pinned me by a men's room door one evening after a CBMC event in 2003 and challenged me to get more involved, to join the National Board. They were seeking younger men."

He accepted the challenge and hasn't regretted a moment of it. "I've been on the Board most of the past 15 years, serving as chairman for seven of them. We have a chance to shape our ministry, to help in keeping our doctrine pure and staying in God's Word as tightly as we can.

"The Lord has blessed us; we have not gotten off course or taken rabbit trails that would take us off our single-minded focus of our two-fold mission – having a heart for the lost, coming alongside a man, then seeing him grow and mature in Christ, in keeping with Colossians 1:28-29. We keep that in the forefront, even though there are so many distractions in Southern California."

Having seen the impact of his father's longtime involvement in CBMC, Mark affirmed the ministry's continued emphasis on reaching out primarily to men. "When you win the heart of a man, you usually get his wife and kids as well.

"We build on the principle of Proverbs 27:17, 'As iron sharpens iron, so one man sharpens another.' It speaks to the power of encouragement, pulling guys together. The same applies to Hebrews 10:24-25, 'And let us consider how we may spur one another on toward love and good deeds. Let us not give up meeting together, as some are in the habit of doing, but let us encourage one another – and all the more as you see the Day approaching.'

"We're part of a group of guys who are like-minded, kind of a fraternity that's centered around Jesus Christ. One of the things I have loved about the ministry is meeting a guy where he is, encouraging him to become what God wants him to be. And I've learned God doesn't waste our pain; He uses our own challenges and development to encourage and share with others."

Reflecting on his extensive involvement in CBMC over the years, Ron observed, "It has provided a real growth opportunity, but discipling men has always been my key calling. I've really appreciated the training CBMC has provided and being able to utilize all the materials the ministry has produced for making disciples.

"CBMC has been an important part of my life since 1960, a wonderful investment in things that really matter. Even at my age, 85, I'm still meeting with men in *Operation Timothy.*"

He affirmed his unwavering enthusiasm for the ministry, even in a time of increasing opposition to the Gospel. "I really believe in the focus we have in CBMC right now. We're not trying to reach the masses — let's be honest, here in California, the masses aren't too interested in what CBMC has to offer. But we have the tools and training for guys who want to go much deeper, in their faith and in their personal ministry. It's better to get 10-12 guys who are really committed to the work than to have 100 guys who come and go, not wanting to get very involved."

Before departing from his earthly life, Ron spoke proudly of his wife of more than 60 years, Marlene, as well as their eight grandchildren and two great-grandchildren. Marlene, who had suffered from disease that caused degeneration of cells in the brain, died weeks after her husband's passing.

Ron noted he was especially excited to see the impact of CBMC being extended into yet another generation. Mark's son, Dane, has been applying some CBMC strategies in his own ministry to people in the world of the arts and entertainment.

"It's called Stage and Story, showing people in the arts how to tie things of the Lord in with the creative work they do," Ron said. He was happy to see the vision of Isaiah 60:22, "one shall become a thousand," being lived out within his own family.

Chapter 10 –

Marketplace Ambassadors

"We are therefore Christ's ambassadors, as though God were making his appeal through us." – 2 Corinthians 5:20

Shakespeare's classic play, "Romeo and Juliet," had Juliet famously asking, "What's in a name?" For CBMC, it has turned out there is a lot in a name. For many years those initials had stood for Christian Business Men's *Committee,* but as the 20th century was coming to a close, that term was causing confusion and consternation.

Early on, "Committee" had served the ministry well. Initially represented groups of Christian businessmen coming together to offer spiritual solutions for desperate times in their cities. In these committees, needs and strategies were discussed and each member accepted specific responsibilities.

Words are dynamic, however, changing in meaning. Over time the word evoked images of tedious, time-consuming meetings rather than people passionately engaged in urgent, unifying causes, such as taking the Gospel of Jesus Christ to business and professional men. The recurring question, "Why 'committee'?" lacked a justifiable answer.

With the onset of the 21st century came fresh looks at CBMC – its image; what teams looked like and how they functioned; its biblical role, and its relevance and appeal for a new generation of business and professional men.

One of the *First Steps* was to redefine what "CBMC" represented. After considering a variety of options the National Board and other leaders, guided by then-President Pat O'Neal, in 2005 settled on Christian Business Men's *Connection.* The common practice of establishing connections to start, build and expand business, seek jobs and address other needs gave the term a natural fit. For CBMC, however, "connection" had much deeper meaning.

It hearkened to CBMC's long-standing mission statement, "To present Jesus Christ as Savior and Lord to business and professional men; and to develop Christian business and professional men to carry out the Great

Commission." To fulfill this calling required a genuine, growing connection with God, making connections with other men to share the Good News of Jesus Christ, and men connecting with one another as followers of Christ to help one another grow spiritually.

To visually capture this concept, a new logo was adopted as well. CBMC's original logo had consisted of a microphone and the motto, "Broadcasting the Gospel," reflecting its initial approach to ministry. That had given way to the symbol of two silhouetted men carrying briefcases, representing businessmen going to tell others about Jesus Christ, as well as one man helping another grow in his faith. However, changes in culture and symbolism rendered that logo obsolete.

An image of three interlocking persons became CBMC's new logo, uniquely signifying a number of elements that were common to the mission. O'Neal explained it represented the Trinity of God the Father, Son and Holy Spirit. It also stood for the Spirit overseeing the spiritual relationship between a disciplemaker (Paul) and a disciple (Timothy). It reflected three men joined in an accountability relationship, as well as one man connecting another man to Christ, who in turn connects another man to Him.

As CBMC took steps to refine teams of men that met weekly for Bible study and prayer, the logo came to represent another innovation. To continue the theme of "connection," the traditional term *committee* was replaced by Connect3 or C3 team. This served to give a sharper focus for the groups, serving as a reminder of the essentials for: a man staying connected to God; men connecting with one another for mutual support and encouragement; and men banding together to carry out the Great Commission and help others discover the joy of becoming connected with God through His saving grace and mercy.

This did not end the process of reexamining what CBMC was and should be, however. One development actually came out of a vivid dream a CBMC staff leader had. Steve Casbon, then the National Director of Field Ministry, awakened one night armed with a vision for men in CBMC seeing themselves as "marketplace ambassadors." This divinely inspired idea was based on 2 Corinthians 5:20, in which the apostle Paul declared, "We are therefore Christ's ambassadors, as though God were making his appeal through us. We implore you on Christ's behalf: Be reconciled to God."

Casbon excitedly worked to develop this idea and engaged a good friend, Mark Whitacre, in his thinking process. The more they and other CBMC leaders talked about this, the more convinced they were that it summarized the urgency of CBMC's mission. Out of the discussions emerged a description of what men in CBMC should strive to be: "We are ambassadors for Christ in the marketplace living out our faith in authentic life-on-life relationships."

This led to specially designed gatherings that became known as the Marketplace Ambassador Initiative, initially with Whitacre serving as the primary speaker. At these meetings CBMC's "DNA" of evangelism and discipleship could be fleshed out and presented to men God might be leading to become personally involved.

In preparation for these meetings, CBMC leaders engaged in numerous discussions to describe and define what a Marketplace Ambassador is. "What are the attributes of a Marketplace Ambassador?" they asked. Starting in 2013, more than 70 possible attributes were listed, each biblically based, but these were gradually whittled down, Whitacre said. Ultimately, the 46th version, "10 Attributes of a Marketplace Ambassador," was adopted in 2014:

1. *Walking daily in intimacy with Jesus Christ.*

2. *Living in accountable relationships with believers.*

3. *Sharing faith in Christ within my sphere of influence.*

4. *Helping others grow spiritually through life-on-life discipleship.*

5. *Living an integrated life with proper life priorities.*

6. *Living a life of generosity.*

7. *Applying Biblical principles in all areas of my life.*

8. *Maintaining a standard of excellence with integrity.*

9. *Genuinely caring for people.*

10. *Living out God's call on my life.*

The first four Attributes, Whitacre explained, related to CBMC's unique mission to evangelize and disciple business and professional men, while the remaining six addressed what someone resolving to live out these biblically based characteristics would look like.

In 2015, the first Marketplace Ambassador Initiative (MAI) was launched in Tampa, Florida at a luncheon where the Attributes, along with principles from CBMC's original *Living Proof* evangelistic training series, were introduced.

At the time, there were four or five CBMC groups in the Tampa/St. Petersburg area. Fruit from the Initiative was almost immediate as it served as a catalyst for rapidly expanding the ministry in the area, moving from a few dozen men actively involved to more than 200, including many in their 20s and 30s.

Whitacre used that as a prototype to conduct MAIs in more than three dozen other cities where CBMC already existed, to cast new vision and expand the ministry there, then began taking them into new areas. He eagerly embraced his role as the Marketplace Ambassador champion, but as his CBMC responsibilities increased another CBMC veteran, Victor Dawson, joined with him to conduct Initiatives in cities where new interest was developing.

This enabled them not only to multiply the number of overall presentations, but also to plant seeds and build excitement in cities where no CBMC ministry had existed. To equip men for the mission, the 10 Attributes of a Marketplace Ambassador, chapters from *Operation Timothy*, and *Living Proof* each provided content for discussion. Men would share openly from their lives, pray for one another, and pray as well for people within their unique spheres of influence.

Connect3 teams became an important means for bringing men together to embrace the vision of CBMC and its mission for reaching and discipling others in the marketplace. In Oklahoma City, Stan Steffen became one of many examples.

Steffen had committed to Christ as a boy, and in college enjoyed a support group of fellow believers at Oklahoma State University. But as an adult, although he had "good Christian friends" and was active in church, "I seemed stalled. I had grown a little dry in my Christian walk. My church involvement didn't seem to translate to the real world."

The owner of a commercial construction company, he had attended the city's Metro Prayer Breakfasts, but knew little about CBMC beyond that. That changed after his first encounter with a C3 team in 2017. "I was hooked. I couldn't help being attracted like a moth to a flame. I got recharged, looking forward to each meeting like a breath of fresh air."

What particularly impressed him was the level of honesty and openness, along with being immediately accepted by other members of the C3 team. Soon after becoming a regular participant, Steffen started taking a man through *Operation Timothy*. "I was a little reluctant at first, wondering how do I mentor a younger man? But in *Operation Timothy*, I found CBMC has a fantastic lesson plan and program for discipling another person."

Having been married for nearly 40 years, Steffen could draw from experience to help the young mechanical engineer who was trying to cope with professional issues as well as the emotions and challenges of being newly married.

"We talk through a lot of things, but I don't advise him on what to do. I just try to help him in the decision process. Going through *Operation Timothy* together, it's amazing how our lives and the passages we're studying so often coincide. And he teaches me so much as well. It's a fantastic opportunity going through the series, talking about being ambassadors for Christ and taking His light wherever we go."

Steffen said the support of his C3 team meant a lot following the passing of his father, and then his father-in-law within weeks of each other. "The prayers and support I received from them – God showed Himself so real, so faithful through them. My relationship with these guys has become vital and has meant so much to me. And now I'm being able to give back to others."

These connections have illustrated a New Testament passage, 1 Thessalonians 2:7-12, describing the intimacy of people united by faith and mission: "but we were gentle among you, like a mother caring for her little children. We loved you so much that we were delighted to share with you not only the Gospel of God but our lives as well, because you had become so dear to us.... For you know that we dealt with each of you as a father deals with his own children, encouraging, comforting and urging you to live lives worthy of God."

His wife, Shelly, observed the positive changes in her husband and often expressed her appreciation for the value of his participation in the weekly C3 sessions. "It's gotten to the point that if my alarm goes off in the morning and I'm not moving right away, she'll nudge me to get going. She's seen the great difference it's made in my walk and how I relate to her.

If I tried to quit going, she wouldn't let me!"

Sam Pappas, president of a civil engineering firm in Edmond, Oklahoma, found his introduction to a C3 team equally meaningful, to the extent that after several months he determined to start one in his own company.

He had been seeking a way to integrate his faith within the company in meaningful but inobtrusive ways. "I wanted to do something to help people here grow in the Lord. I wanted to be aligned with where I sensed God was leading me."

Like Steffen, his first contact with CBMC was through Oklahoma City's Metro Prayer Breakfast. Then he was invited to attend a Connect3 team meeting led by Marty Hepp, the head of another engineering firm. Pappas participated in that C3 team for about three months, until he decided to start one at his own business.

"Before my involvement with C3, I would have said I was accountable and transparent with others. But I discovered a level of trust with these men I had never experienced. If you confessed sin or an area of struggle, there was zero judgment. They were just there to pray for you and help in any way they could."

An added benefit, he said, was discovering mentors for how to run a business God's way. "I could watch the other guys and see how they run their companies. They were blazing a trail ahead of me, and it was encouraging to see that they're still learning, too."

After starting a C3 team at his own company, Pappas saw the same kind of openness develop there. "We have a total of 20 people who attend, 12-14 on any given week. Four of them work here, and the rest come from other industries. We start with prayer, then have a lesson, going through CBMC's *Living Proof* or working through content from *Operation Timothy*. We break into smaller groups for discussion, and then pray for each other. Our focus is always on Christ and the Scriptures."

As a C3 team leader, Pappas committed to meet once a month with Hepp and Brent Vawter, CBMC's Area Director in Oklahoma City, to discuss ideas for building and strengthening their teams. Meeting with them provided yet another encouraging resource for growth spiritually and as a leader.

"This past year, I've grown more personally than in the previous 10 years combined," he said. "I tell my wife, Tracy, a lot of the things I'm learning and she's seeing changes God has done in me through C3, so she definitely supports me in CBMC.

"Through these relationships I've learned to be more open and transparent, and as I love on other people at work – sharing the love of Christ with them – it's changing our company from the inside out. I never want to force my beliefs on somebody, but when the opportunity arises, I tell about what God has done in my life. I want them to know that He loves them as well."

Business owners and high-ranking executives like Pappas and Hepp also could understand the value of being able to meet with peers on a similar leadership level to interact on issues they face every day. To address this need, CBMC introduced Business Forums, later referred to as Trusted Advisor Forums or Peer Advisory Groups.

In the late 1980s, CBMC had introduced Forums into the ministry, where groups of business owners and senior business leaders could meet for several hours once a month. They would provide mutual support and encouragement; offer wise, biblically based counsel as a "Christian board of directors," and united as like-minded men seeking to deal similar challenges in their corporate roles.

The popularity of Forums expanded over the years, and Don Hoffert, an area director for CBMC Northland, became an integral part of that growth. "In reality, we tend to listen to peers before we listen to anyone else. That's not a bad thing," he said, "especially when those peers are focused on glorifying God – living for Him and working through His power."

Hoffert, personally involved with Forums since 2008, observed the impact firsthand as a member of one of those groups. "I've seen transformational spiritual development when a man gets across a table from 10 other men in his group who are working with similar companies and serving in like capacities. In this trusting environment, when a man comes with an attitude of being submissive to God, we see Him do powerful things in lives.

"Offering confidentiality, trust, friendship, mutual support and long-term accountability, these become unique environments for God to work, transforming both heart and mind."

Issues discussed with uncommon candor range from marriage difficulties to workplace challenges to personal struggles, he said. "Once a man is able to confront and deal with what he's been struggling with, we usually see rapid growth in areas that at one time overwhelmed him."

Kent Kusel, working alongside Hoffert in CBMC's Leadership Institute, later called Trusted Advisor Forums, observed how vital a resource like Forums can be. "Senior business leaders – such as company presidents, CEOs, COOs and business owners – are even more likely to go it alone than other guys. Many of them lack anywhere to turn for godly counsel and have few places where they can find wise, biblically based answers for their questions. Decisions they make, which affect the lives of lots of people, are typically made in isolation.

"The saying, 'It's lonely at the top,' is true for many of these executives," he said, "and they're very particular about how they give up their time. Many times they're surprised to learn they're not alone as they encounter other leaders in the marketplace that share a faith in Christ and a desire to serve God through their companies."

Kusel could attest to the impact of being part of a group like Forums. "When I became a follower of Christ, I became a changed man, but was at a loss in how to relate my faith to the workplace. I had never found anyone who could give me a clue about how my faith fit with my business, so I lived a compartmentalized life for years.

"I was pleasantly surprised to learn the Bible had something to say about work. For me, it was almost like being born again – again – as I learned what it meant to be an executive as a Christian."

He pointed out why Forums have become perhaps more important than ever. "In our country we used to be guided by a Judeo-Christian value system, even in business, but those days are fast becoming history. So, as we grow, one man at a time, one team at a time, it has been exciting to see what God can do with 10-15 men together, fired up for Jesus Christ as they direct their companies."

Chapter 11

A Tale of Two (Very Different) Cities

*"They preached the Gospel to that city and made
many disciples." – Acts 14:21*

There's no limit to what can happen when God touches the heart of a man or a group of men. Their families are influenced with the Gospel, along with the places where they work, their neighborhoods, even their cities. Over the years, numerous cities have been positively affected by the presence of CBMC in their business and professional communities. Many could be cited, but consider as Exhibits A and B: Oklahoma City, Oklahoma and Fredericksburg, Virginia.

These two cities differ in size, demographics, and region of the country. Oklahoma City for many years has been a staffed city for CBMC, meaning it has had one or more full-time field staff to help with training men and developing the ministry. Fredericksburg, without full-time staff, has grown through the visionary leadership of dedicated volunteers working as a team. This, we could say, is a tale of two cities. Different, but also very much alike.

CBMC in Oklahoma City traces its history to 1960, with Andy Cornelius often credited for being its original catalyst. Initially, as with other cities, CBMC's ministry took on a variety of activities. In the early 1980s, however, its mission began taking on a much sharper focus under the leadership of men like Dr. Herman Reece.

A maxillofacial surgeon, Reece had a burden for reaching business and professional men with the Gospel message. He cast a vision for Oklahoma City's first metro prayer breakfast in 1983, and continued guiding it when he moved into a CBMC staff role in 1984. The event grew to become one of the premier prayer breakfasts in the county, annually attended by 1,200 people.

Steve Trice, founder of Jasco Products, one of the largest and fastest-growing marketers of consumer electronic accessories, home electric, and security/surveillance products, was one of many whose lives were touched by God through the breakfast.

In 1991, he attended a CBMC prayer breakfast where Bob Vernon, then chief of the Los Angeles Police Department, shared the Good News of Jesus Christ. "I had prayed to receive Christ in two different evangelical churches in the past," Trice said, "but once again I prayed to ask Christ into my life, hoping at some point maybe my prayer would be heard and my life would truly change. My life looked good on the outside, but I was mentally and spiritually dying."

God answered his prayer, but not exactly as he had expected. "Within a couple of hours of returning to my office, two men I didn't know paid me a visit to follow up on my having checked the box on the card at the breakfast indicating I had prayed 'the prayer.' One of these men was Herman Reece, who helped me nail down that decision through prayer.

"He then asked if I would meet with him so he could help me begin learning how to know and follow this Jesus I had just prayed to receive. I told him I was very busy and did not have time for another meeting, but he asked what I was doing the following Wednesday morning at 6:30. When I said I had no excuse for not meeting at that time in the morning, he replied, 'Good. I will meet you here in your office!'"

As an oral surgeon, Reece was a busy man himself, but found meeting with this new believer important enough to add an early morning appointment. This impressed Trice.

"Think about it, a doctor – a successful professional man – with a full schedule had come to see me without an appointment, overcame my reluctance to meet with him, and offered to come to my office at a ridiculously early time just to invest in me! And he didn't do this just once – he met with me Wednesdays at 6:30 a.m. for the next four years."

After that, Trice began meeting with Dan Williams, an executive with a large insurance company in the city, another CBMC member who had a strong background with The Navigators. Reece passed the baton to Williams, who continued to meet with Trice regularly over the next 12 years. "That was a total of 16 years and approximately 800 one-on-one meetings with two men who took time out of their already-packed schedules just to invest with me," he marveled.

This was not casual fellowship. It was very intentional, structured time. "Both men literally poured their lives in Christ into me within the context of the Holy Scriptures. They taught me how to truly follow Jesus, holding me accountable for hearing, reading, studying, memorizing, meditating on and applying God's Word to my daily life," Trice said.

"They asked me the toughest of tough questions about my activities when no one is looking. I learned to trust them with my deepest thoughts and concerns. They helped me identify my primary sin issues, anxiety being most predominant. They had me memorize and learn to meditate on and pray through specific Scriptures that spoke directly to my anxiety issue and the biblical solutions for it.

"As we lived life together, we were able to help each other see our own blind spots – the dumb stuff we think and say that seems right to us but can have a devastating effect on our relationships with others, especially on our wives and children"

Trice continued to meet regularly with both men, although the relationships changed over the years. "And now I am doing the same thing for others that they did for me. I am meeting individually with six men I am discipling just as I was discipled, through the CBMC process we call *Operation Timothy*."

A passage that proved especially meaningful to him in this context was Hebrews 10:24-25, "And let us consider how to stir up one another to love and good works, not neglecting to meet together, as is the habit of some, but encouraging one another, and all the more as you see the Day drawing near."

"True encouragement comes when people like Herman and Dan truly understand our position of desperation and then act upon it," Trice stated.

Drawing from his own experiences, he discovered the importance of following up on people indicating spiritual interest, as well as helping new believers begin to grow in their faith. "How many 'converts' do we have out there who don't really know Jesus?" he wondered. "I think we (the Church) are trying to mass produce Christians, but I'm passionate about the way Jesus did it. He spoke to the multitudes, but had a small group of 12 and also met with a much smaller inner group of three. He lived with all of His disciples 24/7 for three years, walking life together."

Trice, who became a leader for CBMC both locally and as a member of the National Board, said he couldn't overstate the influence of CBMC upon his city. "It's had a tremendous impact. The Metro Prayer Breakfast is kind of a treasured jewel in our city. Last year, for example, the governor attended and spoke. Attendees included our mayor, at least one of our state's U.S. senators, members of Congress, the police chief, fire chief and other officials. We come together to pray for our city, the nation, business leaders, and always have a quality outreach message presented."

In addition to the annual Metro Prayer Breakfast, three more events in Oklahoma City were added to the calendar, designed for both evangelism and discipleship. One was the annual Salt & Light Award Dinner, honoring civic leaders for service consistent with Matthew 5:13-16, which exhorts believers to be salt and light to the world around them. Between 600 and 700 people have attended this dinner every year.

An annual prayer retreat brings men together for spiritual enrichment and prayer, often with a cross-cultural emphasis. At a golf tournament in the fall, CBMC members are encouraged to bring "pre-Christians," not only to participate but also to attend a dinner afterward where prizes are awarded and a speaker brings an evangelistic message.

"We draw from those two events, like a funnel, and as people respond to the Gospel, we invite them to a Bible study, a Connect3 group, or Young Professionals group. From those groups we encourage men to get into a one-to-one discipling relationship," Trice said. "The ministry is really rolling here with a lot of one-on-one discipling going on."

Harold Armstrong can also attest to the impact of the Metro Prayer Breakfast, but in a different way. "I had been asked to do one of the prayers for the Metro Prayer Breakfast, so I decided if I was being invited to pray, I better get acquainted with the organization sponsoring the event.

"I attended follow-up training for the first time. I had struggled with what the word 'discipleship' meant. When I got home, I told my wife, Linda, I had just been exposed to what discipleship is all about."

Dan Williams had used the "hand" and "bridge" illustrations in describing one-on-one discipling. "He showed those diagrams and began rattling off Bible verses as I had never heard a layman do before," Armstrong said. Williams then invited him to go through *Operation Timothy*, which showed him firsthand what the disciplemaking process was like.

Inspired, he began praying for a man he could begin discipling, "to pass on what Dan had done in my life." In 1999, God led him to a man in his church who desired to be discipled. "It was a great experience, and that began a string of one-on-one discipling relationships I have had ever since."

In 2002, Armstrong was contacted and told CBMC was looking for someone to fill an opening on the local board, and Armstrong agreed to serve. When the board decided in 2006 to add another area director, Steve Trice and others encouraged him to consider the role.

"Steve was very insistent, saying, 'Why don't you and Linda pray about it.' The more we prayed, the more I realized that was where my heart was," said Armstrong about accepting the position. He is now Senior Area Director for CBMC in Oklahoma City, although Herman Reece continues to participate in the ministry.

Brent Vawter, the newest member of the city's staff team, had some familiarity with discipling prior to being introduced to CBMC, although he would not have used that term. While attending a church in Tulsa, he had begun meeting regularly with another man for spiritual support and counsel.

"Greg Boyd walked up to welcome me to the church and invited me to have coffee. For the next three-and-a-half years we met regularly, but he never used the word, 'discipleship.' Greg invested in me, helping me to find answers for tough questions, how to hear God's voice and to know His will.

"Then in May of 2011, after I moved to Oklahoma City, I was invited to attend the First Thursday CBMC Prayer Gathering. There I met Harold Armstrong, who told me what CBMC was all about. He became another man who invested in me, and at his encouragement I started discipling another man using *Operation Timothy.*

"At first it seemed intimidating. Several times I thought, 'This is messy,' but *OT* provided a path I could follow. It established a foundation we both could build on. And it gave me the comfort of having a process to work with, a trail that had been well-trodden by many men for decades. I found it to be biblically sound material that keeps you from having to be an expert."

Vawter then attended CBMC's Leadership Coach Training, "and I learned the importance of asking really good questions. One of the things I discovered is you don't have to have the answers – you just help people to ask and explore the right questions for themselves."

It wasn't long before he realized he had made a CBMC connection years earlier. "In 1988, I had attended LeTourneau University, and R.G. LeTourneau's book, *Mover of Men and Mountains,* was required reading. Then in 2012, at a CBMC event in Minneapolis, Minnesota, I met his son, Roy LeTourneau."

The reason Vawter had been invited to the meeting in Minneapolis was because Armstrong and Steve Trice had begun grooming him for a staff position. It gave him an opportunity to get acquainted with what God was doing in CBMC from a broader, nationwide perspective. "At the time my wife, Paula, and I started praying about it. God didn't say 'No' – He just didn't say 'Now.'"

He did accept a staff role in 2017, and "Brent has done a good work in stretching us," Armstrong noted, by bringing new emphasis on attracting younger men to the ministry through Young Professionals teams. To complement this focus, he has initiated a social media campaign, using resources like Facebook, LinkedIn and Twitter, along with a posting every business day called "Character Matters," which talks about godly character traits.

OKC also distributes the "Fax of Life," a weekly email that uses writings from a variety of authors that address everyday workplace topics. About 5,300 people receive it every week.

Marty Hepp, another volunteer leader, working with Armstrong and Vawter, has been instrumental in introducing the Connect3 concept for teams that meet each week. "Four years ago, Marty, who heads a civil engineering team, learned about the Connect3 concept. He was very committed to building leaders within his company, so he went through CBMC's leadership training and started a C3 team in his company," Vawter said.

"He became like an arsonist, a fire starter – he lit the fire for four of our biggest C3 teams, and out of them others have grown. Today, Marty and I partner in helping to lead the teams."

Today, five groups follow the Connect3 format, while nine others meet weekly as traditional CBMC teams. Three other teams meet every week in Tulsa, about 100 miles away. Vawter meets with each of the groups at least once a quarter, participates in the First Thursday Gathering, oversees a quarterly in-reach to keep leaders connected, and coordinates two YP groups that meet regularly.

Armstrong expressed his excitement about what God is doing through CBMC in his city. "We feel like the table is set and we're ready to go for a banquet. Out of each team there will be some who go through *Operation Timothy*, with the 'Timothys' eventually growing to become 'Pauls' themselves and starting to disciple others."

He said reading Phil Downer's book, *Eternal Impact,* made a lasting impression. "In the book he said success is the feeling you get when you reach your goals – but significance is making a difference in the lives of people over time. And that's what we're striving to do when we take another man through *Operation Timothy*. I never get tired of meeting with guys – everyone you meet with is different."

CBMC's history in Fredericksburg doesn't go back nearly as far as that of Oklahoma City. Although it had been in existence for some years, the northeast Virginia community's ministry wasn't fully launched until the early 1990s. That was after a newcomer to the city, Bill McAvinney, attended his first outreach meeting in 1989.

Ted Curtas, a businessman and longtime CBMC member, was the speaker and McAvinney recognized this was the kind of strategy he had imagined for reaching men in the business and professional world for Christ. "This is what I've been trying to find!" he declared to his wife, Ginny, when he got home from the event.

For the next year and a half, he met with a local CBMC group that included Jim Ostrander, a key leader, and a handful of other men. In 1991, McAvinney attended a CBMC men's conference in St. Louis, where Dr. Howard Hendricks was the keynote speaker. It was his first exposure to CBMC on a national scale and he went home impressed.

The next year McAvinney brought nine other men to the conference, and "the third year, 30 of us went." CBMC in Fredericksburg was reborn. "The men before me had been doing an annual outreach prayer breakfast, so I planned one and a guy named Ted DeMoss came in to speak. He was president of CBMC at the time. I had not met Ted before – and that is a story in itself. But he spoke and I quickly learned how God used him as a speaker. It was unbelievable, and that became my real entry point to CBMC."

Since then the ministry has grown to five Connect3 meetings each week, with men studying the Bible and praying for lost men as well as for one another, along with eight Trusted Advisor Forums that meet monthly. Upwards of 100 men are regularly involved with CBMC. The leadership prayer breakfast has continued for more than 35 years. In addition, several "missionaries" have been sent out by the Fredericksburg teams as men took new jobs in several areas, including Nashville, Tennessee and Alaska.

When McAvinney was presented with the city's 2019 Prince B. Woodard Leadership Award, he explained his drive and inspiration. "My motivation is to serve my Lord through my business appropriately, professionally, ethically and relationally. It's to have a good reputation among all and to help people in their life pathways, whatever that might be. The Christian Business Men's Connection has taught me how to live a life of servanthood in the business world and to care about others more than myself."

Even though McAvinney took on the national role of CBMC president in 2017, the local leadership in Fredericksburg remains volunteers, with only a part-time administrator to coordinate major events and help keep men engaged in the ministry. Many of the leaders are true "satisfied customers" who have personally experienced its impact.

Steve Goss was introduced to CBMC in 1995. While attending a Bible college, a dean had helped him to recognize he could pursue full-time ministry in the business world, as well as from a pulpit or in a foreign mission field. "It was like God saying, 'I have placed you where you can share the Gospel while you are working. I've put you there. Now stay the course and be faithful to it.'"

Joining McAvinney and others at a CBMC national leadership conference in 1996, "I saw CBMC was much more than I realized it was. Being around men from all over the U.S.A. and learning about the history of CBMC, I wanted to be like those men, to be able to share my faith in the same way."

Goss has been active in Forums with other business leaders since 2002, a group of six men holding one another accountable, discussing each other's challenges, and offering mutual support and counsel based on the Scriptures. "I haven't missed a month since."

He meets with several men in *Operation Timothy* each week, having taken more than 10 men through it over the years. "One of them did not even know the Savior when we first met. He just wanted someone to walk life with him. Most of the guys I've met with have caught the vision for sharing their faith and meeting with other men."

"CBMC has been absolutely wonderful for me. It's been an encouragement to know thousands of men across the country share the same vision and passion. Attending the CBMC World Convention in Orlando, Florida in 2014, I saw business and professional men from around the world with the same heartbeat."

As a member of the CBMC leadership team in Fredericksburg, Goss said, "We're able to share with each other biblical principles for business, we study the Word of God, encourage men to pray for others, and hold ourselves accountable to one another. Our desire is to be more effective in leadership and to listen to God's Spirit through the Scriptures."

Goss said he is often approached by young entrepreneurs wondering, "How do you serve Christ in the marketplace – how can you live this out?" His response is, "It's incarnating the truths and principles we're trying to communicate as we disciple and invest in others. Ephesians 3:20 says God is able to do far more than I can think or ask, and over the past 30 years, I've found that's so true."

Art Scanlon attended his first CBMC prayer breakfast thinking it would be a good way to make business contacts. He never suspected he would be hearing someone speak about the business of eternity.

"When I arrived, I felt what I needed was business. But then I heard the speaker's testimony; I had never heard anything like that. By the end of the meeting I was silently saying to God, 'All I know is I'm for you. I hope You're for me.'"

Months earlier Scanlon, a hotel manager in Fredericksburg, had received a phone call from Bill McAvinney, who was seeking a venue for an event he was planning. That led to an invitation to the 1997 prayer breakfast where Scanlon marked his registration card, indicating he had prayed to receive Jesus Christ.

"Bill followed up on me and invited me to meet with him for a Bible study. We started in early November and proceeded slowly. It was more relationship-building than anything. When we got to the section of *Operation Timothy* that asked whether I had received Jesus Christ as Savior and Lord, I told Bill I had prayed that at the last prayer breakfast. But now that I had a lot more information about what it meant, I wanted to say it again."

The two continued to meet, and when Scanlon encountered personal challenges, McAvinney was there to lend support, offer counsel, or direct him to others that could offer specific help.

When Scanlon moved out of the area to take a new job, he and McAvinney remained in close contact. "He and his 'CBMC posse' were instrumental in my growth in the Lord while I was in Fredericksburg. When I started working in the D.C. area, my growth, learning and fellowship continued with a new group of CBMC men."

Some years ago, Scanlon started coordinating special outreach meetings for people in the hospitality industry, modeled after CBMC events he had attended. "I wanted to reach out to people who do what I do, and see somebody be touched for Christ the way I was.

"Even though I'm in the meeting planning business, I'm not a meeting planner. So, in 2012, when I felt called to do a prayer breakfast for peers in the industry, I decided to 'cut a deal' with the Lord. I told Him if he'd bring me a speaker, then I'd do the breakfast."

Not long afterward he met Mark Whitacre at a breakfast meeting. "Mark told me he was doing a lot of speaking for CBMC, including some upcoming events in D.C. I asked if he'd be willing to speak at the prayer breakfast I was planning. We agreed on a date and he became our first speaker."

This initial outreach turned into an annual event, Scanlon said. "We've seen a number of people drawn closer to the Lord, and several have come to Christ. It's been very rewarding to see some of my peers in the industry also experience the joy of knowing Christ."

When Ron Riblet moved to Fredericksburg in 1989, he was looking to expand his bread and baked goods distributing company. Early one morning he went to a local restaurant for breakfast and saw a group of men meeting, so he decided to join them. "I crashed a CBMC breakfast prayer meeting," he chuckled.

That would be the first of many breakfast and lunch meetings Riblet has participated in since then. Along with attending weekly CBMC prayer meetings, about 18 years ago he became a member of a Trusted Advisor Forum. "I could see CBMC's two-fold purpose being worked out in both groups, so when the first Forum was started in our area, it made sense for me to buy into both of them. As an independent business owner I didn't have a Christian board of directors, which drew me to Forums in the first place."

In both formats, along with praying for the spiritual needs of others, he has benefited from the wisdom of other Christian business and professional men with expertise in using the Scriptures in the workplace. "I gained a lot of valuable spiritual counsel and business advice I could not have gotten on my own," Riblet said.

Since 2010, he has been dealing with chronic heart failure, which was diagnosed at the Mayo Clinic. Health issues, however, have not diminished his zeal for CBMC or his participation in its mission.

"When I was in the hospital, the Holy Spirit would impress on me to pray for somebody in the heart wing of the clinic, maybe to talk with them or just lift them up in prayer, and this led to many opportunities to talk with them about Jesus Christ."

Prior to his diagnosis, Riblet had gone through *Operation Timothy*, and after returning from the Mayo Clinic he began taking an attorney through *OT*. "Tom said he had observed something different in me, a sense of peace he hadn't seen before in someone he actually knew. He couldn't understand how I could have such peace in spite of my circumstances.

"We know that God has the days of our lives numbered, so we know that each new day we have is a blessing. So when 'tomorrow' turns into today, it's an opportunity to share that blessing with others."

Over the years, despite having a heart functioning well below capacity, Riblet has been a quiet, behind-the-scenes leader in CBMC whom God has used to touch many lives both directly and indirectly. He, like so many others, is bearing fruit that will last.

Tim Golike learned about CBMC in 1999, having been invited to attend an event in Fredericksburg. A commercial airline pilot, Golike wasn't able to attend weekly CBMC meetings consistently. In 2007, however, after starting a construction business, he heard about Forums for the first time. "Being a new business owner, I felt they had something that could really help me, so I was able to join one in early 2008.

"These were godly men who helped point me in the right direction with business, personal and family issues I was dealing with. I could go to them for counsel, and they wouldn't provide me with answers, but would offer suggestions based on what the Scriptures teach."

In 2014, when there was a need to start a new Forums group in Fredericksburg, Golike volunteered to lead it as a moderator while remaining involved with his other group. "Once you make great relationships like that, you don't want to let go of them. These were my Trusted Peer Advisors, and we met in a setting where guys can really open up and speak in confidence with one another."

He was also a member of Fredericksburg's local CBMC leadership team for a number of years. "I have easily appreciated the fact that our purpose has always been focused on evangelism and discipleship. I have several Timothys going on, all in different stages of their spiritual growth."

Golike said, "Even though I don't have the gift of evangelism, I like CBMC's emphasis on lifestyle evangelism. It provides tools I can use, both in sharing my faith and in discipling other men."

When he turned 65 in 2018, he had to retire from United Airlines due to age requirements. He viewed that simply as the start of a new chapter. "I'm excited about the fourth quarter of my life. I don't want to be sitting on the bench; I want to be out there on the field."

Part of Golike's vision was to move to Anchorage where his daughter lived and get a job there as a pilot, since age limitations in Alaska are less restrictive. However, he also realized, "God has to be – needs to be – more important than any dream that I have."

His goal was to continue being involved in CBMC there and help to expand the ministry, where two Forums were already established, as well as a weekly Bible study.

Several men in Fredericksburg have learned that when tragedy strikes, they can count on their brothers in CBMC. Among them was Fred Brown, who lost two teenage grandsons from injuries suffered in a car accident as they were driving to school on a foggy morning.

While Brown and his family grieved over the loss, friends from his Forums group and CBMC weekly prayer group came alongside to offer comfort. They coordinated a memorial service for the boys in the largest church in the area, which was filled to overflowing. "So many men from CBMC showed up to support us," he said.

The day after the service, Brown's Forums group met as scheduled, but set aside the planned agenda. "I wasn't the speaker, and didn't intend to be, but all the guys stepped back and let me talk. They listened and offered support, and briefly shared about some things that had happened in their own lives."

Their support continued for months afterward, Brown noted. "We received many cards from my brothers in CBMC. My wife, Kendra, read them all and was really touched and encouraged by them. It was a terrible thing that left a big hole in our lives. But our friends gathered around us and we knew God was with us the whole time."

Receiving this kind of support was not new for Brown. Five years earlier his business was going through some challenges. "I needed some Christian men to talk with. I felt like I had given everything to God, but hadn't given Him my company. My shoulders weren't broad enough to carry that load.

"At the time I would have told you my life was all about business. Today, thanks in large measure to CBMC, my life is all about faith. My faith in the Lord has grown tremendously, and I know God put us all together for a reason."

Ken Hinkle, owner of a construction company, agreed about the power of spiritual support available through CBMC. He came to appreciate the value of Forums so much that he agreed to moderate two of the groups. "It's an opportunity to share successes and failures with other businessmen, becoming a family of men growing in their concern and open sharing with one another.

"It seems when things are going well, everybody wants a piece of the action – but when you're doing poorly, good friends can be hard to find. With our Forums groups, you know you have someone to turn to and they can turn to you."

Is the Bible relevant for the ever-changing business and professional world of the 21st century? These and many other men in Oklahoma City, Fredericksburg and hundreds of other cities across the United States would give a hearty answer of "Yes!"

Chapter 12 –

Enough Ministry for a Lifetime

*"...my only aim is to finish the race and complete the task
the Lord Jesus has given me – the task of testifying to the good news
of God's grace." – Acts 20:24*

As this book is being written, CBMC is preparing to commemorate its 90th anniversary. Through the years its activities have changed, but from the start it has consisted of Christian business and professional men devoted to God, to one other, and to the ministry of helping others experience a new or growing relationship with Jesus Christ. How has this happened? In our transitory world, when today's fascination quickly fades into the shadows of history, how has CBMC – founded in 1930 – endured, thrived, and remained true to its calling?

Certainly, CBMC has enjoyed the grace and anointing of the Lord. Another factor has been individuals who recognized CBMC as God's special calling on their lives and stayed faithful to that call for a long time.

CBMC has been blessed by many such men, some already introduced through these pages. Countless others could be singled out, well-deserving of mention. Since it would be impossible to mention everyone, here are just two more examples of faithful men – we could call them "lifers" – who have invested decades of their lives to the ministry of evangelism and discipleship through CBMC.

Don Hull of Cleveland, Ohio could be counted among those described earlier as "satisfied customers." A corporate attorney for more than 30 years, he first got involved with CBMC in 1965, six years after marrying his wife, Linda. He would take her to church on Sunday mornings, then head for the golf course. "We were married in a church, and I did get to see Linda baptized, but that was it," he said.

The turning point came when a businessman invited Hull to lunch and talked with him about Jesus Christ. "I listened to what he had to say, trying to understand, and about eight weeks later I prayed to receive Christ. He took me to my first CBMC meeting in Tulsa, Oklahoma and there I met Max Webb, a veteran CBMC leader."

Hull began attending CBMC meetings regularly and became chairman of the downtown Tulsa group before taking another job in Pittsburgh, Pennsylvania in 1972. He became involved with the North Hills group, eventually becoming its chairman, and then helped to start a new group in downtown Pittsburgh, serving as its chairman as well.

In 1975 he was introduced to a new CBMC tool called *Operation Timothy*, not long after Joe Coggeshall began introducing it across the country. "I had heard of *Operation Timothy* and the need to make disciples, but was not convinced," Hull admitted. "So, I agreed to try it one time."

His first "Timothy" was John Stock, a former professional football player who had been a Christian only about a year. "John's football career was over and he was working as a salesman. He was very receptive, and in the years since he's probably discipled more men than I have," Hull said.

The third stop on his CBMC tour around the country was Cleveland, where the ministry dated back to the 1930s, not long after the ministry's founding in Chicago. "We had been to Cleveland before, in 1973, when the CBMC national convention was held there. Linda and I drove over from Pittsburgh. Jimmy Carter, then Governor of Georgia, was the speaker at an outreach luncheon held in conjunction with the convention."

When Hull moved there, the Cleveland CBMC group was holding weekly Bible study and prayer meetings at a city mission with paper tablecloths, "not a very conducive setting for businessmen. I asked the group if they were doing outreach and was told they hadn't done that in a couple of years. So, we scheduled our first outreach luncheon in 1985."

Next, he and several other executives teamed up to organize the city's first mayor's prayer breakfast in 1986. "We had 1,500 people in attendance, and Sam Rutigliano, former head coach of the Cleveland Browns, was the speaker. That really gave CBMC here a boost. We missed a couple of years, but we have had 28 of those breakfasts since then. We now call it our Leadership Prayer Breakfast, with great speakers and a large turnout each time."

When CBMC's introduced the Metro 80:80 program to start the 1980s, local leaders in Cleveland caught the vision for having multiple groups – then called committees – in the city's metropolitan area. They actively started recruiting young men into the ministry.

Having been involved with CBMC for more than 50 years in Tulsa,

Pittsburgh and Cleveland, Hull said it became "the driving force in helping me to be intentional about being an ambassador for Christ, as 2 Corinthians 5:20 tells us. I have appreciated the question, 'Are you a tourist, or are you intentional?'"

Some churches, he said, because of an emphasis on foreign missions, distinguish between those who are "called" to ministry and those who are not. "I have even heard the message, 'Be a sender or a goer.' But the Bible teaches we all have an impact on others. Our unique spheres of influence make us insiders with them, including in the marketplace, where we work and spend so many waking hours. Most of us spend more time there than in the neighborhoods where we live.

"CBMC brought home to me the concept of discipleship, being fellow workers in the Gospel – we are God's fellow workers, as it says in 1 Corinthians 3:9."

Hull observed that when he was introduced to CBMC, it was largely an evangelistic ministry. "The emphasis was on soul-winning, and Ted DeMoss always told us to 'think lost,' to keep our focus on people outside the body of Christ. And I believed that. He spoke for me at CBMC events in Tulsa, Pittsburgh and Cleveland.

"Then Joe Coggeshall came along and stressed making disciples. He said we shouldn't take a man off our prayer list after he gets saved – he's just getting started (spiritually). Joe helped us to become intentional about making disciples, as Jesus taught in Matthew 28:19-20."

Hull shared a story to illustrate the urgency of reaching out to others for Christ and helping them to grow spiritually. A speech writer in the public relations department for a major oil company in Cleveland came to Christ late in life. Soon after becoming a believer, he saw a magazine ad for a men's Bible study being held every Wednesday. It was a CBMC group Hull was leading.

"Victor arrived about 45 minutes late and asked if that was the Bible study he had read about in the ad. He apologized for being late, saying he had to attend an open house from 7 to 8:30 that morning. He and I soon started going through *Operation Timothy* and met every week, even though we lived 45 minutes apart. We were almost finished, when he died of a heart attack. Soon after his passing, his widow called me. We had never met, but she asked if I would speak at his graveside service at Queen of

Heaven cemetery.

"About 75-100 people jammed under a tarp since it was raining that day. I spoke after the priest and gave Victor's testimony, how he had come into a personal relationship with Christ and that I knew he was now in heaven. In Tulsa I had been a public defender for several years before entering corporate law, so I explained about how his and my criminal records – our sin – had been wiped out, erased by Jesus' sacrifice on the cross.

"After the service we all went to the widow's house for a meal, and a couple of lawyers I had not known previously wanted to talk about what I'd said."

Even in his 80's, Hull has been taking men through *Operation Timothy*. "Two of the men I've been taking through *OT* have already started taking others through, even one that was only a few weeks into it himself. This speaks to the fact that a businessman can have a ministry no matter where he is in his walk with Christ."

Hull talked about "E-squared" – "evangelism to the lost and the edification of the saved" – and expressed his excitement about how God has caused the work of CBMC to flourish in metropolitan Cleveland and northeastern Ohio.

"More than 25 years ago we started catching the vision for what the Lord wanted to do here, we have a full-time staff guy, Steve Conzaman, who has been with us for several years. We also have a growing CBMC ministry in the Akron area, which Mark Whitacre helped get started through the Marketplace Ambassadors Initiative. Steve is providing leadership there as well."

Tom Sommers of Fresno, California has remained active in CBMC for well over 30 years. He explained the reason is simple: because of what it has meant in his life and the impact the ministry has had in the lives of others.

Sommers had walked the aisle of a church to declare his commitment to Jesus Christ, but kept God on the periphery of his life during his early adult years. After recommitting his life to Christ in 1985, he attended his first CBMC meeting in Fresno at the invitation of a friend. He then began going through *Operation Timothy*, which launched his walk with the Lord.

Prior to the CBMC luncheon, he said, "I had not had a Bible in my hands for over 20 years." Because God had rekindled his faith through CBMC, Sommers became involved with the ministry, taking on leadership roles, always with a heart for young men in the workplace. In 2010 he became an area director, stating, "Working with CBMC, I'd call it a labor of love – but it's not work!"

The influx of younger men becoming involved in Fresno has been especially encouraging, Sommers said. "We have about 55 'young stallions,' men who are 40 and under, who gather each week for prayer meetings, and seven 'super stallions' – between 25 and 40 years of age – who also meet at 6 a.m. once a month for Bible study." He explained early morning meetings, starting at 5:30, work best for many of these men since the time doesn't conflict with work responsibilities, and after work they are eager to get home to their families.

Equally exciting has been the shifting demographic of CBMC in the Fresno area. When Sommers first became involved with CBMC, he said it was primarily white and members were mostly older business and professional men. Today, participation reflects the mixed ethnicity of the Fresno area, along with a much younger cross-section.

As with his own life, when CBMC helped him reconnect with God after many years adrift spiritually, he has witnessed countless examples of rebirth and renewal that have rewarded patience and perseverance. The *Living Bible's* translation of Proverbs 21:5 states, "Steady plodding brings prosperity; hasty speculation brings poverty," and to Sommers, this is a key to CBMC's effectiveness. "This principle doesn't just apply to finances."

One recent example is a former professional athlete in his 60s who had not been to a church since he was five years old. He was unreceptive to anything "religious," yet over the years had remained close to his high school coach, a strong follower of Christ.

When the one-time athlete's mother died at the age of 90, Sommers and the coach came alongside him to offer consolation and support. "I had known him, too, since he was a boy. We told him about an all-day Bible study seven of us had been conducting once a month, including other men involved in sports – two coaches, two pro athletes, an umpire and two businessmen.

"We invited our friend to join us, and he accepted," Sommers said. "About a year ago he prayed to receive Christ in our CBMC office. He continues to meet with our group every month, and he and I are going through *Operation Timothy*. He asks very good, deep questions, and because of the close relationships we have in our Bible study group, we have excellent discussions filled with respect, no matter what he asks. This is what steady plodding is all about."

The virtue of persistence, he said, has application for people of all ages, not just those who are approaching the latter stages of their lives.

"A few years ago, a businessman I mentor asked if I could meet with his 33-year-old younger brother who was just coming out of an 18-month recovery program. I agreed to do so, and he and I have been meeting every two weeks, 6-7 a.m. at our CBMC office. I listen, he talks. He has accepted Christ and has been free from substance abuse for the first time in many years. He also attends a men's Bible study at his church and is experiencing a whole new life."

When God touches a man's life, Sommers pointed out, it affects those around him, including his family. He cited the example of a man he had known for more than 20 years. "He got married 15 years ago but had walked away from the church. About 10 years ago he got into alcohol and drugs, his marriage was in shambles, and he was wrestling with lots of anger.

"Some months ago, I asked him to join our weekly Tuesday morning Bible study with five other men – and to my surprise, he accepted. He has been with us every week since, has begun attending church again, his marriage is much improved, and again exhibits a softness about him I had observed when we met two decades ago.

"I gave him a Bible – he had never read the Bible, even though he had attended church for years. I recall being thrilled when he memorized three verses, the first time he had ever done that. His dad, a very close friend of mine, sent notes telling me about the new person he was seeing in his son."

Effective ministry to men is not complicated, according to Sommers. It's a matter of being faithful, available, and genuine. "I reach out to a ton of guys of all ages, seeking to share the Gospel with them. I don't hit guys over the head with it; I just try to get to know them and let them know I care. All you have to do is listen and let them do a lot of the talking."

He makes a practice of calling 25-30 men nearly every day, many he has known from the past and has not heard from in some time. "I just let them know I was thinking about them and care about them, too. If they don't answer the phone, I leave a message. Sometimes they call back even a year later, asking why I had called them.

"In 1 Corinthians 15:58 it says, 'be steadfast, immovable, always abounding in the work of the Lord, knowing that in the Lord your labor is not in vain.' The lesson is simple: Don't give up on your friends. Keep connecting – and throwing out seeds."

Chapter 13

Transitions in Leadership

*"To everything there is a season, a time for every purpose
under heaven." – Ecclesiastes 3:1*

In 1991, CBMC had a new president for the first time in 14 years. Ted DeMoss, who had assumed the role in 1977, took on the role of president emeritus, but stayed very much a part of the ministry to business and professional men. He remained in high demand as a speaker across the country, continued serving on the National Board of Directors, and maintained his evangelistic fervor, inspiring others wherever he spoke.

This initiated a series of transitions in which men whose lives God had touched through CBMC took on the top leadership role and each in his own way helped to advance the ministry through their respective gifts and experiences.

Succeeding DeMoss was Phil Downer, an attorney from Atlanta who, with his wife, Susy, also an attorney, had been introduced to Jesus Christ through CBMC. Having also been discipled through *Operation Timothy*, he knew firsthand the impact the ministry could have in the life of a man and his family.

A gifted speaker who had honed his skills through courtroom litigation, Downer proved a popular successor to DeMoss, presenting his powerful testimony from coast to coast. He had served in combat as a Marine in Vietnam, experiencing the horrors of war, and when he spoke communicated effectively how that and other traumas had influenced his life prior to his encounter with Christ.

After going through *Operation Timothy*, he had proceeded to disciple others and served as a living example of the power of spiritual multiplication and commitment to making disciples to the third and fourth generations. Downer's spiritual journey reflected how discipleship can and should be the culmination of the relational process that evangelism often is. He captured this truth in his first book, *Eternal Impact*.

With Susy, they represented the power of ministry as husband and wife. They would speak at couples' outreach events, and would meet with couples together in going through *Operation Timothy*. As their children got older, they often joined them in speaking at events where CBMC couples attended, including family conferences. The Downers challenged other couples to minister together in their homes and neighborhoods.

As national conventions started losing momentum with the changing business culture, Downer introduced weekend men's conferences as means for bringing together men from different parts of the country to enjoy mutual encouragement and learn from each other how to engage in evangelism and discipleship more effectively and fruitfully.

In 2000, Downer left his CBMC role and started another discipling ministry, which ultimately enabled him to minister more directly to veterans of the armed forces who, like himself, had dealt with the challenges of Post-Traumatic Stress Disorder (PTSD).

Fritz Klumpp, who also had served during the Vietnam War, except as a jet fighter pilot for the U.S. Navy, was appointed to succeed him. A retired pilot with Delta Air Lines who also had worked part-time in the real estate business, Klumpp had served on CBMC's National Board but always approached his new role as serving on an interim basis. For that reason, rather than using the term President, he preferred the title of Executive Director.

A graduate of the U.S. Naval Academy, he had received the Distinguished Flying Cross for his "heroic and extraordinary achievement in aerial flight" during a mission against enemy installations in North Vietnam in April 1966. During that mission, Klumpp's jet was shot down and he was rescued just off the Vietnamese coast. Over the course of the conflict, he flew a total of 136 combat missions and earned numerous other commendations.

Years later, while based in the New Orleans area as a Delta pilot, he and his wife, Ann, began attending a Sunday school class taught by a former semipro baseball player who could relate to Fritz. This person was instrumental in their coming to faith in Christ, and Klumpp then started attending CBMC meetings and going through *Operation Timothy*.

He served on the National Board and became a trainer for both CBMC's *Lifestyle Evangelism Seminar* and the *Living Proof* training series, helping others to discover the underlying biblical truths for personal, relationally based evangelism, and equipping others to lead the programs.

As CBMC's Executive Director, Klumpp's primary focus was to

strengthen relationships with ministry leaders across the country, both in staff and volunteer roles. He championed the motto, "The power of one God, the value of one man, to the third and fourth generation." This underscored the impact an individual could have on many lives when empowered by the Holy Spirit.

When Klumpp decided to step aside in 2004, he was succeeded by Pat O'Neal of Raleigh, North Carolina, a real estate developer. Like his predecessors, O'Neal was a product of CBMC, coming to know Christ after attending an outreach meeting and being discipled through *Operation Timothy*.

He became actively involved in CBMC locally, taking on leadership roles, and then was asked to serve on the National Board. Then, after being named President of CBMC, O'Neal continued the emphasis of interacting with key leaders across the country, seeking to ensure their ideas and concerns were carefully considered.

Under his leadership, CBMC's Legacy Leadership Initiative was started which later became known as Leader Advancement Training. One of the innovations was development of leader/coach training, equipping both staff and volunteer leaders to effectively utilize a coaching style for leading rather than the common approach of telling people what to do.

O'Neal recognized the need to reach out to the next generation of business and professional people and get them involved in the ministry. This strategy included the introduction of another revision of *Operation Timothy*, a larger formatted, graphically enhanced edition which came to be known as the Signature edition.

Another change involved the renaming of CBMC groups, shifting from the outdated "committee" terminology to become Connect3 (C3) teams. This represented connecting with God, connecting with one another, and connecting with other people for the sake of the Gospel. This included a vision for reproducing teams every three years to help in multiplying the ministry.

He also encouraged taking CBMC tools and strategies to other parts of the world, with staff men like Paul Johnson of St. Paul, Minnesota and Chuck Whitmore of Baltimore, Maryland joining him to expand the vision for reaching the business and professional world for Christ.

In 2009, O'Neal was succeeded by Lee Truax, who also brought a CBMC pedigree as he assumed his new responsibilities. His father, Ernie Truax, has served as an Area Director for many years, including Rochester, New York, Pittsburgh, Pennsylvania, and New England. After years as a local volunteer leader, in 1994 Lee began serving as a Ministry Associate in the Boston metropolitan area and had a long connection with the CBMC Family Camp at Schroon Lake, New York.

He had established a successful career as an executive in the technology industry, and as President brought this knowledge and expertise to CBMC, promoting a new digital approach for evangelism, discipleship and training.

Paul Johnson, having the perspective of serving in staff roles with both CBMC and CBMC International for more than 30 years, commented on innovations Truax helped to introduce.

"He had a vision for digital delivery of the tools and resources, recognizing we were operating within an increasingly digital age and needed to be cutting edge," Johnson said. "He wanted CBMC to develop a digital warehouse, continually developing tools and growing over time, then making them accessible via the Internet."

This served to extend CBMC's impact to many parts of the world, with its digital resources being used by people in more than 70 nations. These included videos, *Operation Timothy*, sermons and messages, making those tools available for people virtually anywhere in the world.

Under Truax's leadership, the Marketplace Ambassador Advancement System and the Marketplace Ambassador Initiative were introduced, with Mark Whitacre emerging as its primary champion. The "10 Attributes of a Marketplace Ambassador" were formulated, with leaders and C3 teams using those for weekly discussions and application to their own roles in the everyday workplace.

Presentation of these concepts also served as a vehicle for introducing more men to the work of CBMC, especially younger and emerging business leaders. Truax completed his tenure as CBMC President in 2017, leaving a legacy of leading CBMC's march into the digital world and expanding its global reach.

He was succeeded by Bill McAvinney of Fredericksburg. While he had been a follower of Christ before being introduced to CBMC, the ministry had intersected with the course of his spiritual journey from his youth. He had attended the LeTourneau Christian Campgrounds in Canandaigua,

New York (as recounted in the Foreword), and then learned about CBMC when he attended his first outreach as an uninvited guest in Fredericksburg.

He and a small team of other men worked to revitalize the CBMC ministry in that community about 50 miles outside of Washington, D.C., he was named to the National Board and served as Chairman, Vice Chairman and Treasurer for many years. From the start of his tenure as President, he has emphasized remaining true to CBMC's longtime purpose statement, "To present Jesus Christ as Savior and Lord to business and professional men, and to develop Christian business and professional men to carry out the Great Commission."

McAvinney also has encouraged the expanded use of the Young Professionals for engaging men in their 20s and 30s through their own Peer Advisory Groups. His philosophy of leadership and special areas of emphasis for CBMC are discussed elsewhere in this book.

Chapter 14 –

CBMC Enters the Digital World

"...of Issachar, men who had understanding of the times, to know what Israel should do." – 1 Chronicles 12:32

Over the 20th century's last two decades, technology transformed communications in ways never imagined. With the aid of satellites, a new national newspaper – *USA Today* – was created. FedEx introduced next-day mail delivery. Electronic mail, quickly shortened to "email," streamlined business communications. The "World Wide Web," later embraced as the Internet, brought immediacy and easy accessibility to virtually any kind of information.

CBMC was very methodical in adopting this revolutionary technology. But by the early 2000s, the time for evaluation was over. Its value and importance were indisputable. The moment for moving forward had arrived.

Its first website was little more than an online brochure, as was the case for many organizations just discovering the capability of new technological resources. However, with the addition of staff people having expertise in both traditional and digital communications, more aggressive advances could be made.

One of those additions was Phil Stone, a former sports broadcaster who brought a background in interviewing and video production. Under his guidance, cbmc.com soon moved from static online images to expanded content, cutting edge graphics, and videos and podcasts to communicate with very visually oriented audiences.

These communications were utilized not only through the website, but also via email and other means for delivering challenging and inspirational messages in tight, impactful packages.

Under the leadership of then-President Lee Truax, who had worked with Hewlett-Packard, Compaq and other technology companies, CBMC explored even more powerful means for better equipping its men for the mission of evangelism and discipleship in the modern-day workplace. For help, he turned to Mark Hofert, who had been invited to join the CBMC leadership team by Truax's predecessor, Pat O'Neal.

Like Truax, Hofert came from a computer technology background, having retired after a successful career with IBM. He had been introduced to *Operation Timothy* through a men's Bible study in Libertyville, Illinois, a Chicago suburb, then became involved with CBMC in South Florida and then Raleigh, North Carolina, where he met O'Neal.

Hofert spearheaded an initiative to develop a digital environment for CBMC's resources and tools, at first called Integrated Learning Architecture. "It started when a CBMC donor asked if we had the resources, what would we do to extend CBMC's influence in the marketplace," he recalled. "We knew that if we were to grow in an ever-increasing technological environment, we would have to have a significant digital presence."

As the work proceeded, according to Hofert, there was a temptation to go in different directions, "but Lee did a wonderful job of keeping us within our mission." One key decision was that *Operation Timothy* would be a key to the entire process, to be presented in a readily accessible online format.

A software development company in Atlanta assisted with the effort, encouraging CBMC to develop an "ethnography" to clarify what *Operation Timothy* was and how it was being used. Research was done in different parts of the country to better understand the usage of the tool.

"We created an electronic version of *OT* based on these sessions with men across the USA," Hofert said. "It helped us evaluate how it would translate electronically and how we could enhance its use and value. For instance, we found that very few people cover a whole chapter at a time, so we include bookmarking capabilities that can be used by both the Paul and the Timothy.

"The Paul could also keep notes on a particular Timothy that would be private and available only to the Paul. For instance, he could record how he was praying for the man, his marriage and children, his job, and issues of spiritual growth. With both the paper version of *OT* and *eOT* available, it came down to what the Paul and the Timothy preferred."

At the same time, two other key elements were emerging as foundational for the new digital platform. Mark Whitacre and Steve Casbon had introduced the idea of individuals in CBMC being Marketplace Ambassadors, derived from 2 Corinthians 5:20, "We are therefore Christ's ambassadors, as though God were making his appeal through us. We implore you on Christ's behalf:

Be reconciled to God." Whitacre championed this concept, promoting it across the country through Marketplace Ambassador Initiative meetings.

"It became clear that in the marketplace, our mission was to serve as ambassadors – Marketplace Ambassadors," Hofert said. "This ultimately led to renaming the Integrated Learning Architecture, calling it the Marketplace Ambassador Advancement System (MAAS). We wanted to do everything possible to help men in the ministry advance as Marketplace Ambassadors," Hofert said.

A new website, advance.cbmc.com, was created and linked to the original cbmc.com site. In addition to presenting the "10 Attributes of a Marketplace Ambassador," it posed the provocative question, "Are you a TOURIST or an AMBASSADOR?" This highlighted the difference in level of commitment between someone who is just a casual visitor and the person who is serving as an official representative.

Along with *Operation Timothy* and the Marketplace Ambassador content, one more element needed to be incorporated into the new digital platform. In 1991, CBMC had developed *Living Proof,* a video-based series for group training in relational or lifestyle evangelism. Hofert's team worked to update it for online use, and the result became known as *LivingProof Adventure.*

"We wanted to bring *Living Proof* into the new century. The original had excellent content, but it featured highly scripted actors – some Christians and some not – and in some respects the videos had become dated. In our era of reality TV, people wanted to see what's real. At the same time, we wanted to highlight some of the sound principles from the 1990's version," he said.

"The original consisted of 32 videos, ranging in length from five to 14 minutes each, but they were not organized in a way that could be used as a curriculum or learning series. It wasn't as structured as we would have liked. So, we built *LivingProof Adventure* based on those original videos, but using real people and real-life experiences, honing it down to 12 principles of relational evangelism that could be used around the world."

A fourth piece to the digital puzzle, simply called Library, was incorporated to function as a resource center for materials related to evangelism, discipleship and the challenges of serving and representing Jesus Christ in the workplace.

The years of work to bring CBMC fully into the digital world culminated in September 2014 when the website and the electronic version of *Operation Timothy Signature* – also known as *eOT* – were introduced at the CBMC World Convention in Orlando, Florida. From the start, the reception of the new format and updated resources were overwhelmingly positive.

Producing the electronic version of the discipling tool involved more than conversion from printed to digital format. Several changes were made to make it an even more effective tool. For *eOT*, the Leader's Guide was embedded into the system; it could highlight key ideas and provide additional questions for discussion; supplementary resources were listed; and participants could incorporate additional resources, such as books, videos and audios.

Eldon Kibbey, who had been serving on CBMC's field staff team in Indiana for nearly two decades, befriended a man from the United Kingdom at the Convention and they agreed to start going through *Operation Timothy* together. The distance and five-hour time difference were an obvious problem but the introduction of *eOT* became part of the solution.

Besides the new electronic *Operation Timothy*, they employed another technological resource – Skype – so they could meet face-to-face, despite being thousands of miles apart. Millions of people around the world had found Skype an effective and enjoyable way to stay in contact with friends, family members and business associates in other cities or countries. Kibbey and his new British friend realized they could do the same – but with a primary purpose of discipling.

"We started going through *OT* using Skype on Wednesdays, at 3 p.m. for me, 8 p.m. for him," Kibbey said. "Even before *eOT* was introduced, I had found it worked very well with me and the man I was discipling using the printed edition. But it was the first time I had done it with someone overseas, and we found it just as enjoyable and effective."

He referred to this approach as "diskypleship," a term not unique to him. "I learned about a couple of young ladies here in Indianapolis that were doing *Operation Timothy* with other women using Skype. They had pioneered that approach and told me, 'We call it diskypleship.' After that I began using it a lot, but wanted to make sure they got the credit for the idea."

Kibbey observed online discipling quickly became popular among men of all ages. "I was one of several people involved in the pilot orientation training for *eOT*. After working out the bugs for several months, along with adding pieces to it, I became very comfortable with it. One of my Timothys, with whom I had been meeting for a couple of years, was very excited to learn *eOT* was coming. When we had started meeting, he had been typing his answers on his computer, even though he was using the book. So, the electronic format was a perfect fit for him."

Since *eOT* can be accessed on any electronic device, the Paul and Timothy could take their choice of computer, laptop, tablet or smartphone for the user-friendly discipling tool. With younger adults especially tech-savvy, *eOT* immediately opened new avenues for use within that age group.

"A youth pastor at a church where we spoke arranged for fathers to take their teenaged sons through *eOT*. He would meet with the fathers on Saturday mornings, going through a lesson, then over the next week the fathers would meet with their sons and go through the same material. It's exciting to see that kind of interest from young guys who use their cell phones and other devices all the time," Kibbey said.

He found that one's age, however, was not always a determining factor for whether a man opts for the online or print version of *Operation Timothy*.

"I had two young guys, 21-year-olds, I was taking through *OT* using Skype. One of them picked up on *eOT* very quickly, but the other decided he'd rather use the book. Then there was a 30-year-old man I met with who looked at *eOT* and decided he wanted to use the book, and a 58-year-old man who told me he would much rather use the electronic version.

"It's been interesting to see the personalities in play – maybe that has more to do with which they prefer than generational differences. Other factors can come into play as well, such as the reality that sometimes people may forget or lose their books, but they always have their smartphones on hand."

One additional benefit is how *eOT* can help in fulfilling Christ's call to go into all the world and make disciples. Kibbey said he had a friend doing global evangelism using an online program, ministering to many people in Africa. He lacked a good discipling tool for following up with them, so when he heard about *eOT*, he was eager to put it to use.

With *eOT* being available at no cost, there is no economic barrier when reaching into impoverished areas, and no shipping is involved. "The price is right for people in other countries," Kibbey said.

Having served as the lead in the development and release of *eOT*, Hofert wanted to try it out and see firsthand how it was received. Jeremiah, a friend who was a web designer, was the perfect candidate. He agreed to go through *Operation Timothy* with Hofert, and they began meeting once a week at a restaurant in Durham, North Carolina.

They would arrive with laptops or tablets under their arms and work through the questions. After they had been meeting for more than a year, Jeremiah's company transferred him to Asheville, about five hours away.

"I told Jeremiah I didn't want to stop meeting, but knew we couldn't both drive five hours each week to get together either," Hofert said. "So instead, we started using Skype – or occasionally, FaceTime – to continue our weekly meetings. From the start, it was great."

This was their first experience with diskypleship – discipling via Skype. Hofert explained being able to see each other as they were going through each chapter of *Operation Timothy* online, rather than just hearing each other over the phone, helped them continue having in-depth, heart-to-heart discussions, whether related to work or other challenges Jeremiah was facing.

When business brought him back to the Raleigh/Durham area, Jeremiah would continue to meet with Hofert in person. However, the virtual face-to-face sessions definitely enhanced their discipling relationship and removed the geographical obstacle.

"We don't meet as regularly now," Hofert said, "but we stay in contact and I've been greatly encouraged by what I have seen the Lord do in his life. I'm praying he'll soon find a man in his own life that he can start discipling."

Hofert noted the diskypleship approach is just as useful when frequent travel for the Timothy or the Paul makes in-person meetings on a consistent basis difficult or impossible. "In discipling someone, meeting in person only every three or four weeks won't be very effective. So, Skype or FaceTime sessions when either the Paul or Timothy is on the road can be an excellent substitute.

"It's amazing how technology, coupling the *eOT* format and resources like Skype, can enhance the discipling process and overcome an unnecessary hurdle."

Chapter 15

Communicating the Mission
of the Movement

"Consequently, faith comes from hearing the message, and the message is heard through the word about Christ." – Romans 10:17

From the start, CBMC utilized communications media to good advantage to enhance its mission to take the Gospel to the marketplace. The first noon-hour evangelistic meetings in Chicago were broadcast over radio stations to expand the impact of the messages, reaching many who could not attend the events due to time or distance.

Radio continued to be a favored medium through the years, not only in the metropolitan Chicago area but also in many other parts of the United States. In fact, CBMC adopted the motto "Broadcasting the Gospel" for its logo and for a long time displayed it and the image of a radio microphone on lapel pins designed for suitcoats.

Testimonies from large community prayer breakfasts, as well as brief, 1-2 minute inspirational messages by a variety of CBMC leaders, have been broadcast over both Christian and secular radio stations with good impact.

TV programming, utilized to a lesser degree, also has shown to have similar effectiveness. In metropolitan Philadelphia during the 1980s, then-Metro Director Larry Kendrick collaborated with Tom McDowell, a CBMC member who directed marketing for a local TV station, to produce a half-hour program, "Man to Man." It aired Sunday mornings for seven years, featuring businessmen who shared their testimonies about how they came to know Jesus Christ and explained the difference their relationship with Him meant in their lives and careers.

CBMC also used the printed word extensively both to communicate the Gospel message and to encourage and challenge members in the strategies, resources and opportunities available to them.

Claes V.S. Wyckoff, later a San Francisco advertising executive, became the first editor of *Contact,* work he did from his home in Evanston, Illinois. Its name was derived from the descriptive mission statement: "contact with God in prayer for wisdom; contact with other Christian men for fellowship; contact with churches for service; contact with men who need Christ; contact with radio audiences for a wider ministry, and contact with servicemen for witness and fellowship."

Several times a year, special issues of *Contact* were devoted to "Personal Experience," telling the testimonies of business and professional men. Other editions concentrated on CBMC events and tools being developed to enhance the ministry of evangelism and discipleship in the marketplace.

In 1981, Robert J. Tamasy left a 10-year career as a newspaper editor to become editor for CBMC and later its director of publications. *Contact* was one of his responsibilities and in 1984 he guided a refocusing of the magazine from stories of how men had come to know Christ to a more topical publication, offering a biblical perspective on everyday workplace issues such as stress, decision-making, leadership, risk-taking, teamwork, personal finances, unemployment, and time management.

This shift in content made the magazine a pacesetter in the Christian world, offering not just a theological perspective but also real-life stories of committed followers of Christ who were dedicated to living out their faith through their companies, in their offices, and through their travels across the United States and around the world.

Directed primarily to members and participants in the ministry of CBMC, many of the readers commented on how much they benefited from articles and columns that clearly communicated how relevant and practical the timeless principles of the Bible were for applying their faith in Christ at work and in their everyday lives.

Publication of *Contact* ceased at the end of 1997, but the void it left for showing what the Bible teaches about contemporary business concerns was filled in part by "Monday Manna," a weekly workplace meditation created and distributed by CBMC International. Initially it was distributed via fax every Monday morning, and later through emails. Over time it began reaching many thousands of readers around the world, being translated into more than 20 languages.

Numerous books have been written by and about men involved in the CBMC ministry, ranging from R.G. LeTourneau's autobiography, *Mover of Men and Mountains,* to DeMoss's account of his life and ministry, *The Gospel and the Briefcase.* David R. Enlow captured the first 40 years of CBMC in *Men Aflame,* and *The Complete Christian Businessman* and *Jesus*

Works Here, both edited by Tamasy, were compilations of articles that had first appeared in *Contact Quarterly* magazine. Phil Downer's book, *Eternal Impact: Investing in the Lives of Men,* was a significant contribution to the Christian men's movement of the 1990s.

Several of those books later were translated into other languages, including Korean, Chinese, Spanish and Dutch.

"When I joined the staff of CBMC in 1981, there was very little in terms of writings available to Christians about how to integrate their faith in the workplace," Tamasy said. "There were only two Christian books directed to business and professional people, and one of those had been written by a pastor. Over the succeeding years there was an explosion of faith-based business books, and CBMC helped to lead the way with work it published in both magazine and book formats."

As noted in other chapters, CBMC became adept at the use of evolving technology such as videotape presentations, then DVDs, for the *Lifestyle Evangelism Seminar, Living Proof: Evangelism* and *Living Proof: Discipleship.* Later CBMC began using digital media, including the Internet to make available an extensive array of ministry resources. These have included *Operation Timothy, LivingProof Adventure,* leadership, coaching and mentoring training, podcasts, personal testimonies, announcements of upcoming events, and many other tools on its cbmc.com website.

When it comes to conveying an important message, there is no substitute for direct, face-to-face communications. For this reason, conventions, conferences and retreats have always been an important element of CBMC's teaching and training ministry.

The first CBMC Convention was held in 1938 at the LaSalle Hotel in Chicago, when 150 men from across the United States gathered for mutual encouragement and inspiration for their quest to reach more businessmen for Jesus Christ. Over three days the attendees assembled for prayer, Bible studies, morning and afternoon training meetings, and outreach.

Conventions became an annual event the next year when men gathered in San Francisco, beginning their sessions on a fateful day, Sept. 1, 1939, which marked the official start of World War II. At first the conventions were for men only, but eventually that changed with wives being invited to join their husbands and guest speakers including women like Corrie ten Boom, Jill Briscoe, Beverly LaHaye and Joni Eareckson Tada.

Speakers were primarily CBMC members, but keynote speakers of national and international note were regularly featured, including Dr. Billy Graham; Georgia Gov. Jimmy Carter; C. Everett Koop, a Philadelphia CBMC member who later became U.S. Surgeon General; Sen. Mark Hatfield of Oregon; evangelist Luis Palau, Leroy Eims of The Navigators, theologians Dr. Howard Hendricks and Dr. Haddon Robinson, Dr. John MacArthur, Dr. Richard Strauss, D. Stuart Briscoe, and many others.

Programs for each convention included daily Bible messages, music, prayer, testimonies, and workshops that focused on various aspects of the CBMC ministry and introduced new resources.

The conventions continued until the mid-1990s, when they were ended due to declining attendance and a changing culture which made increasingly prohibitive the cost and time expenditure of the meetings, which typically went from Wednesday until Sunday. In their place, national and regional conferences were conducted to continue providing members with the encouragement of like-minded men from across the country, as well as to give training in such important elements as evangelism, disciple-making, team building, mentoring, and coaching.

Regional CBMC family conferences offered opportunities not only for men in CBMC but also their families to receive solid Bible teaching, fellowship, recreation and to join in prayer and worship. Among the settings for these were Covenant College in Lookout Mountain, Georgia (the event was later moved to Lake Junaluska, North Carolina); Schroon Lake, New York; Cannon Beach, Oregon; Sandy Cove, Maryland; St. Paul, Minnesota; Black Hills, South Dakota; Green Lake, Wisconsin; Mt. Hermon, California; New Braunfels, Texas; and Lake Tahoe.

For countless men, women and children, these events proved to be life-changing as they encountered Jesus Christ in new and fresh ways, as well as had opportunities to interact with fellow believers sharing a great passion for serving the Lord and living out their faith in the marketplace. They also provided opportunities for wives to feel more a part of the work of CBMC.

In some instances, the impact of these family gatherings has been felt through multiple generations, as has proved to be the case for the Balinski and the Chetelat families.

Dave Balinski was actively involved with CBMC in West Philadelphia, and he, his wife Cheryl and family attended their first CBMC Family Conference at the Sandy Cove retreat center in North East, Maryland in 1986. They encountered CBMC families from Pennsylvania, New Jersey, Maryland and Delaware, as well as some other states.

"Our two young boys caught the bug. They loved it," he said. "Before this we knew nothing about family camp, but once we went, we were hooked."

Two years later, in 1988, the Balinskis loaded up again for Sandy Cove – this time with an addition, a four-month-old daughter named Dara. It was the weekend of Father's Day, and over time it proved to be a divine appointment.

"A meeting with one CBMC family in particular changed our lives, especially the life of our newborn daughter," he said. "The other family was John and Paula Chetelat, who brought their daughter and newborn son, Scott. Dara and Scott met as 'clients' in the nursery of that family camp."

The bond between the Balinskis and Chetelats continued to grow over the years, with the annual family conferences serving as a traditional meeting spot. Friendships between the children grew and deepened. This culminated on November 12, 2016, when the one-time newborns exchanged wedding vows in Mechanicsburg, Pennsylvania. A little more than 12 months later, Dara and Scott became parents for the first time, welcoming Rebekah Grace and making Dave, Cheryl, John and Paula her grandparents.

"It's amazing, a seed that was planted at a CBMC family camp blossomed into love that led to a wedding and then extended to a third generation," Balinski said.

Balinski now serves as CBMC's National Director of Field Staff and Connect3 Coordinator.

The CBMC conference at Sandy Cove is no longer being held, but another continued in Black Mountain, North Carolina that both families started to attend. That family camp, started in 1920 under the sponsorship of a ministry called Fishers of Men that merged with CBMC, anticipated a centennial celebration for 2020. Over that 100-year span, the conference had been hosted at Covenant College in Lookout Mountain, Georgia, and then at Lake Junaluska, North Carolina, before relocating to the Ridgecrest Conference Center at Black Mountain.

Chapter 16 –

Going into All the World

"Therefore go and make disciples of all nations...teaching them to obey everything I have commanded you." – Matthew 28:19-20

Almost from its inception, CBMC embraced a vision beyond having a local or even national impact. It had expanded into Canada as early as 1941, and during the 1950s the ministry extended its reach to many parts of the world, including Korea, Mexico, Ireland, Australia, and more than two dozen other countries. CBMC leaders R.G. LeTourneau, Theo McCully, J. Elliott Stedelbauer and others, at their own expense, traveled to numerous nations to represent CBMC and its mission.

By the mid-1980s, however, leaders saw the need to reorganize a "loose confederation" of 21 independent CBMC national ministries around the globe into a more structured network for evangelizing and discipling business and professional people.

Ted DeMoss, who accepted invitations to speak for CBMC outside of the United States, was the first to express concerns. He had observed that despite numerous CBMC entities internationally, there was no unity of mission or strategy. Over time, beginning around 1975, many countries had broken from the single CBMC Board and had become independent with their own boards of directors.

Many had lost any emphasis on evangelism and discipleship, turning into congenial fellowship groups with no outward ministry focus. What CBMC looked like in one nation was very different from what could be found in another country. Little follow-up on new believers was taking place. All they shared in common was the name.

CBMC's National Office in Chattanooga, Tennessee had begun hosting representatives from a variety of other countries for training, including Mexico, South Africa, Australia, India, Germany and Holland, but there was no unifying structure to advance a common strategy.

Desiring to instill a new passion for carrying out Jesus' Great Commission for evangelism and discipleship, Ted brought Joe Coggeshall on some of his trips to introduce *Operation Timothy* and explain how it should be used.

However, their efforts to cast vision for disciplemaking were largely unfruitful.

To remedy this problem a two-pronged strategy was proposed: To draft formalized organizational guidelines for CBMC internationally and ask each national board to agree to abide by them; and appoint a new International president to oversee the work globally.

Duane Jacobs, who served as National Director of Administration for CBMC from 1980 to 1984, was asked by the International Board to help in drafting a new constitution and bylaws for a reorganized CBMC International. He enlisted the aid of Jim Welch, an attorney in Lakeland, Florida who was active in CBMC, to guide the documents through legal channels.

Once the Board approved the documents, Jacobs joined with Roger Erickson, who was serving at the time as CBMC's Executive Vice President, DeMoss, Roy LeTourneau and Welch on a search committee for selecting the new CBMC International president. Several candidates were considered, but ultimately Erickson was the choice to head the newly incorporated CBMC International.

"We had 21 countries when CBMC International officially got started in 1987," Roger recalled. "We were pushing for them all to get involved in one-on-one discipleship. My job initially was to make sure the new constitution was understood and get everyone started in evangelism and discipleship strategies. It took about three years for the new name – CBMC International – to be approved by all."

Erickson, who had built a successful career as an insurance executive before joining the United States staff in 1980, was familiar with traveling overseas on behalf of the ministry. His trips for CBMC, prior to assuming the role of CBMC International President, had included Nassau, Bahamas; Hawaii; Acapulco, Guadalajara and Mexico City, Mexico; London, England; Jamaica; New Zealand; Australia; and Santiago, Chile.

However, interacting with CBMC leaders of other nations in an official capacity proved an eye-opener for him. While seeking to impart the vision for evangelism and discipleship in the marketplace, he observed distinctive cultural differences that didn't align with U.S. approaches. Rather than attempting to sway them to the American way of doing things, he conceded, "It's not wrong, it's just different."

For instance, in the Netherlands a group was meeting at a bar near the airport. When Erickson arrived, he was guided into the bar where everyone was sitting, drinking beer, very unlike what he was accustomed to in the United States. On another trip to Jakarta, Indonesia, with his wife, Mary Ann, they found wine placed at every table at an outreach event. Again, quite different from what was standard common practice at U.S. functions.

But he understood his assignment. "I learned about the importance of being able to adjust to the culture, and help them to develop a complementary purpose and plan that would foster evangelism and discipleship."

Erickson served in that role for 10 years, traveling to six continents. His stops included Canada; Rio de Janeiro and Sao Paulo, Brazil; Buenos Aires, Argentina; Philippines; Singapore; India; Holland; several African nations; Denmark, and other parts of Europe.

In 1997, at a CBMC World Convention in Rothenburg ob der Tauber, Germany, he passed the president's mantle on to Tim Philpot, an attorney from Lexington, Kentucky whose father, Ford Philpot, was an internationally known evangelist.

Philpot was speaking extensively at outreach events for CBMC in the United States, and had made several ministry trips to India as well. He began to expand his itinerary, visiting countries on several continents to help in expanding the work of CBMC there.

Under his leadership, a once-a-week workplace meditation, "Monday Manna," was created to encourage business and professional people around the globe in their efforts to represent Jesus Christ. Initially the one-page, biblically based commentary on common workplace topics was distributed via fax, but as soon as it became feasible, CBMC International began sending it out every Monday by email.

This communication became well-received. Over time individuals in different nations volunteered to translate Monday Manna into their own languages for further distribution. In Brazil, a huge, multi-cultural country, enterprising leaders took the initiative to find people to translate it from English into Portuguese, Spanish, Italian, German, French, and later, Japanese.

Philpot served as CBMC International's President from 1997 to 2003. He was succeeded by Robert Milligan, a business owner from Lincoln, Nebraska, and he continued in that role until 2011, when Jim Firnstahl, a businessman from Tucson, Arizona, assumed the top leadership position.

An initiative to keep senior CBMC members engaged in the ministry,

"Operation Levite" began in 2000. The goal was to keep experienced men involved long after they had retired from the business and professional world. The "Levites" changed over the years, but they would meet at CBMC World Conventions, occasionally at other CBMC national or regional events, and take part in quarterly conference calls to discuss developments within CBMC; pray for specific needs; and learn how they might be able to assist in various nations.

A number of them traveled to other countries on behalf of CBMC, seeking to challenge and encourage leaders there in reaching out to unsaved peers in the marketplace and disciple new believers to grow in their faith.

One of the Levites, Charles Miller of Elkhart, Indiana, had actually first encountered CBMC decades earlier while on a business trip in Australia. Miller later became very active in starting a new CBMC group in Elkhart, and later served on the CBMC National Board, so he had a very personal appreciation of the ministry's value around the world.

Today, the ministry of CBMC is reaching business and professional people in more than 80 nations. However, the ongoing growth of the global marketplace made CBMC's task of taking its vision and strategies to other nations and ethnic groups easier. Not only were CBMC members involved in international commerce able to minister during their trips to other lands, but the "mission field" was also coming to the United States.

Albert Diepeveen was a classic example. A native of the Netherlands, he had witnessed the horrors of World War II there as a child. As an adult, he and his wife, Theresa, immigrated to the USA soon after they had married. An entrepreneur, he started several enterprises before finding a niche in computer technology, becoming an early distributor of Apple computers.

As a businessman, Diepeveen came to know Christ through a local church but was discipled through CBMC. Because of the ministry's impact on his life, he became very involved in it, first in his hometown of Bourbonnais, Illinois, and later nationally as a speaker and board member.

Starting in 1981, Diepeveen began traveling to Holland to provide CBMC training, and then was invited to do the same in Portugal. He also helped to connect CBMC with other marketplace ministries in Europe. This led to the creation of Europartners, a consolidation of CBMC, IVCG, the International Chamber of Commerce and other non-profits that ministered to business and professional people.

He became the first Chairman of the Board of CBMC International in 1987 at a World Convention in Vancouver, British Columbia, Canada. He served two four-year terms in that role.

"It was a very exciting time," Diepeveen said. "It was nice to be part of something that was growing, not only in numbers but also in impact, and be involved in leadership. I think I was accepted a little bit more, especially early on, because of my European background.

"We all came to appreciate cultural differences and different ways of doing ministry. CBMC made a major contribution with *Operation Timothy* being translated into many different languages. IVCG had its own style of outreach and discipleship, so we came to realize we could learn from other countries – learning together – and implement the best from each of them."

Fook Kong Li, a businessman who was born and raised in Hong Kong, was another example of CBMC's international flavor within the continental United States, although his time in the ministry was tragically shortened.

A deacon at his church in the Chinatown section of Los Angeles, California, he was greeting guests one Sunday morning in 1985 when a gunman, who had entered the service searching for his estranged wife, fatally shot Li and the church's pastor.

Even though Li's earthly life had been cut short, his legacy continued not only within his congregation but also in the lives and hearts of the many people in CBMC with whom he had ministered, including as a member of the National Board.

Ted Hubbard, a solicitor (attorney) from Bromley, Kent, England, traveled to the United States on numerous occasions, both to speak at outreach functions and serve as an unofficial "chaplain" for CBMC staff across the country. Accompanied by his wife, Gladys, the Hubbards offered wisdom and biblical counsel to couples confronting the challenges of personal ministry and family life. His British sense of humor also enhanced conferences as he brought greetings from "across the pond."

Yet another example of CBMC's intersection with other cultures has been the more recent establishment and expansion of unique Korean-American CBMC groups in several parts of the country.

These ethnic CBMC groups, now under the umbrella of Korean CBMC of North America, have grown to more than 40 in the United States and several in the Canadian cities of Toronto and Vancouver.

Started in 1985, they initially offered Korean-speaking gatherings for first-generation South Korean immigrants (who had come to the U.S. as adults) and "1.5-generation" Korean-Americans who had been born in South Korea but immigrated to America with their parents as children or teenagers. As time passed, second-generation members who had been born in the U.S. to Korean parents also started to become involved.

For nearly 15 years these groups, according to Paul Hyon, president of Korean CBMC of North America, served primarily as ways for Christian business and professional men to make social connections with fellow believers. Over the past decade, however, "we've been trying to refocus our mission and align with that of other CBMC teams across the U.S.A., emphasizing evangelism and discipleship."

Despite some cultural differences, Hyon said, progress is being made to establish "Paul-Timothy" discipleship training through the *Operation Timothy* materials.

Korea's history with CBMC dates back to 1953, when American CBMC leader Cecil Hill introduced the ministry during the Korean War. It was members of CBMC Korea who came to Los Angeles about a quarter-century ago to initiate ethnic groups there.

"Most Korean CBMC meetings are conducted in the Korean language and have some other cultural differences from typical American teams, but we are now exploring how to reach out to the next generation of Korean-Americans," Hyon said.

"I am a direct result of the CBMC progress," he noted. "Sam Hwang, one of our longtime Korean-American CBMC leaders, took me through *Operation Timothy* and I benefited greatly from his mentoring and discipleship. Now I meet with and disciple about three men every week, and we're now at a fourth-generation level of spiritual reproduction."

Hyon, a former banking executive who has been involved in CBMC since the late 1990s, said God "has turned my life around" through CBMC.

"Until encountering men in CBMC, I thought ministry was only for pastors and missionaries. Through CBMC I learned the workplace is part of God's calling. It gave me a totally new perspective, learning about relationship-building through business and work. It has been eye-opening, life-changing."

"At one time I had questioned whether God was calling me to become a missionary or pastor, but CBMC helped me to realize God calls you wherever you are – to serve Him and the people around you."

From its inception – and now more than ever – CBMC has been directly engaged in fulfilling Jesus' command to make disciples of all nations. Sometimes by members going to other parts of the globe, and sometimes by people from around the world coming to the United States and getting involved in CBMC.

Chapter 17

Women and Families – Not Forgotten By CBMC

"…believe in the Lord Jesus and you will be saved, you and your household." – Acts 16:31

Always having a core of Christian businessmen sharing a burden for the spiritual needs of their cities as the Great Depression ground forward, CBMC had a broad vision. However, with the passage of years it became evident that while newly developing ministries were targeting specific segments of society, including children and young people, college students, the military and women, one segment was being either overlooked or ignored – business and professional men.

For this reason, CBMC very intentionally focused its strategies and resources toward reaching men in the marketplace for Jesus Christ. However, this did not mean there was no place for women in the mission and ministry of CBMC.

Among the first examples of this was Edith DeMoss, mentioned earlier in this book. Mrs. DeMoss was a helpmate and partner with Ted DeMoss in many ways, not only raising their three daughters while Ted was traveling across the United States for speaking engagements, but also hosting guests from out of town and opening their home for couples Bible studies. Here is a story about one of those couples:

Two CBMC members, Charley and Bob, were part of an office visitation effort following a Mayor's Prayer Breakfast in Chattanooga in the mid-1980s. More than 1,800 men and women had attended the event, and dozens of guests had marked registration cards indicating first-time commitments to Jesus Christ.

One of the cards was filled out by someone working at a downtown accounting firm. When they arrived, Charley and Bob asked if they could see the guest, whose first name was Terri. As they waited, Bob noted the last name was hyphenated. Since the first name ended with an "i," Bob observed, "I wonder if this is a woman who has combined her last name with her husband's?"

Charley, one of the most kind-hearted men anyone could ever meet, responded, "You think it's a woman? Do you think we should leave?" It wasn't that he did not care about her spiritual needs; he just wondered whether two men calling on a woman in that setting was appropriate.

"No, let's see if she's available and talk with her just as we would anyone else," Bob responded. "She marked her card, so let's see what she thought of what the speaker had to say."

As it turned out, Terri was a female CPA working at the firm. She had enjoyed the speaker's message at the breakfast and acknowledged she had sincerely prayed at the close of the talk. However, plans for her follow-up were already in place.

She and her husband, Rodger, were scheduled to begin a Bible study with Ted and Edith the following week and she was excited to get started. So, Charley and Bob offered further encouragement, giving assurances she would enjoy it, then briefly prayed with her before they left.

Weeks later, Ted recounted an early meeting he and Edith had with Terri and Rodger. "We were in *First Steps*, in the chapter called, 'Is the Bible credible?' Neither she nor her husband had a church background, but were obviously very open spiritually. I asked her to read 2 Timothy 3:16 which says, 'All Scripture is God-breathed and is profitable to teaching, rebuking, correction and training in righteousness.' Then I asked Terri to tell us what that meant in her own words. Almost without any hesitation, she replied, 'This says that God wrote a book!'"

The couple continued meeting with Ted and Edith for many weeks after that, confirmed their new faith and became active in a local church.

Edith served primarily in a behind-the-scenes role, praying for her husband whether he was speaking, leading a training session, or meeting one-on-one with someone needing to hear the saving message of the Gospel. At times, however, she became more directly involved. Ted described an example in a little book he wrote, *Thoughts of Chairman Ted,* when she urged him to invite an unsaved, out-of-town businessman to a CBMC luncheon that afternoon.

Ted recalled he was leaving for an extended trip to California the following morning. He always tried to bring at least one non-believer to every luncheon he attended, but that particular day he'd not invited anyone. "Honey, there's not a way in the world that I could run that fellow down today," he told

Edith, but suggested she could contact the man herself to invite him.

Late that morning, as he was about to leave his office for the meeting, his secretary informed him, "Ted, here's your guest for lunch."

It was the young man he and Edith had discussed that morning. She had called Ted's secretary, who in turn called the businessman, a building materials salesman, at his motel at 10 a.m. He happened to be in his room, having returned to get his umbrella because it was raining. Ted's assistant simply told the man her boss wanted to take him to lunch, so he had arrived 10 minutes before noon.

"At the luncheon, one of my salesmen was giving his testimony for the first time," Ted said. "As he closed his talk, he offered a word of prayer. After the meeting was over, I just turned to my unexpected guest and asked if he was a Christian. He said no, so I asked why he had never accepted Christ. Tears came to his eyes right away.

"He said, 'I'd be a Christian today if someone would just show me how to be saved.'"

Ted immediately explained how to receive Christ as his Savior, and after their brief conversation, the brand-new believer eagerly told several other men at the luncheon he had just prayed to invite Jesus into his life. He and Ted stayed in contact over the years and he remained true to his commitment to Christ.

"It hadn't been my plan for that day. I had to get ready for business and didn't feel like I had the time. This young man was reached for Christ in a way that only God could have put together," Ted stated, including a helpful nudge from his wife.

Many other examples of women who became vital partners with their husbands in the work of CBMC could be cited, but another that stands out was Gladys Coggeshall. She became a spiritual mom for many young wives as her husband, Joe, helped men encounter Jesus Christ for the first time and begin growing in their faith.

Bruce Witt, who served on the CBMC staff in a variety of roles both in Atlanta and Houston in the late 1980s and early '90s, recalled the impact both Gladys and Joe had on him and his wife, Dana.

"Joe and Gladys began discipling us as a couple in 1983. We were originally from Montana, so being 2,000 miles away from home, they became like parents to us. We actually moved in with them briefly while we were getting settled in our new house in Atlanta.

"We would go over and have dinner in their home, just hang out. It gave us an opportunity to get to know and love their family – to observe their lives up front and personal. From a discipleship standpoint, we were able to see the life of faith modeled; it wasn't just about knowing and learning the Scriptures.

"As we watched the two of them together, she really did complete him, complementing his ministry and relationships with others. With Joe's strong personality, apart from Gladys I think he probably would have run people off."

Drawing from their years of experience as a staff couple in the Twin Cities, Ken Johnson and his wife, Ardie, could appreciate the importance of ensuring that new staff men and their wives were in agreement and eager to work in their new city as a team.

"I remember when Max Webb was trying to recruit us to staff, he drove up to a cabin we had in Ely, Minnesota, just to spend time with us," Johnson said. "He just loved us and modeled three things: loving people, being a shepherd, and caring for people. We observed how Max and his wife, Mildred – a very low-key couple – were true shepherds to other staff couples."

Ardie understood the unique challenges wives face when their husbands are engaged in vocational ministry, not only time demands but also the financial pressures of raising support. She had experienced that while her husband served as a director for the Twin Cities, later as state director, and then added more regional responsibilities.

"When a potential staff man was being considered, we would always host him and his wife in our home for two or three days," Johnson said. "This gave Ardie the opportunity to spend time alone with the wife and see if she was on the same page with her husband. We wanted to be certain she was supportive of the work her husband would be embarking on, that she understood the value of CBMC as a men's ministry, and saw the impact it could have on a man's entire family."

He said whenever a question arose about why CBMC focused exclusively on men, Ardie could share her perspective. "She often observed there were many more ministry opportunities for women, even in the workplace, but not nearly as many that were tailored for the unique pressures men face in the business and professional world."

During Phil Downer's tenure as President of CBMC, his wife, Susy, not only supported him but also often traveled with him. They would speak together to couples and she spoke individually at women's meetings. Like Phil, Susy had been an attorney, so she felt comfortable in a public speaking role.

Over the years, women were often invited as guest speakers at national conventions, conferences and retreats. Among them were Joni Eareckson Tada; Jill Briscoe, wife of Stuart Briscoe; Nancy Leigh DeMoss, niece of Ted DeMoss; and couples like Bill and Anabel Gillham, David and Teresa Ferguson, and Jack and Carole Mayhall of The Navigators.

Women have always been welcomed at major events like community prayer breakfasts and outreach meetings. However, in terms of one-on-one discipling and group meetings, such as Connect3 teams, Forums and other Peer Advisory Groups, a men-only policy has been observed with good reason.

CBMC President Bill McAvinney explained, "the process of really getting to know a person's heart in a spiritual discussion can often lead to vulnerable and emotional interactions. We believe that if a man and woman (not his wife, girlfriend or relative) were to engage in a very personal discipling relationship, it could lead to unintended consequences.

"And I'm sure most wives wouldn't react very favorably to news that her husband was meeting regularly with another woman to help her grow in her Christian faith.

"However, we wholeheartedly encourage couples to minister together with other couples, actively engaging in a like-minded exploration of their faith and what the Bible teaches," he said. "The history of CBMC reveals many remarkable stories of a husband mentoring another man while their wives were meeting together in a similar spiritual journey."

For many women, what they value most about CBMC is how it has helped their husbands become men of godly character, in the home as well as the workplace.

Aimee Mestler attested to the impact CBMC has had on her husband, Derrick, as well as their family. She said he had been very successful in business, but when he became involved with CBMC in Fredericksburg, Virginia, "it was like new life was breathed into him. It gave him a new purpose for life, and now he's focused on ministry to other people.

"Derrick has always been a precious, godly man, but now the support he has through CBMC, it's like the Christian piece has been added to his career."

In 2014, the Mestlers attended the CBMC World Convention in Orlando, Florida, and that greatly expanded their vision for how God could use them in reaching out to others in the marketplace.

"Some men in Fredericksburg paved the way for us to attend with our children, and we were blown away by what we experienced at the convention. We met people from all around the world, and that reinforced our desire to be a part of what God is doing through CBMC," Aimee said.

While homeschooling their two daughters, she had been hosting women's Bible studies in their home, and desired something like that for her husband. "I was so excited to see a group of men encouraging each other as they do in CBMC. Having a place where he could share all the ups and downs of life really solidified Derrick in having the support and camaraderie with other men at the early morning breakfasts."

His primary mentor became Bill McAvinney, and that relationship extended into their family. "I've really appreciated how Bill checks in on our family regularly. He's provided a sweet, fun-loving accountability and support for my husband."

At the World Convention and other CBMC events, Aimee enjoyed gaining new friendships. One of those was with Ken and Vonnie Hinkle, another couple from Fredericksburg. "Even though she was undergoing treatment for cancer, Vonnie still poured into me when we were going through some hard stuff at our church. I knew she was dying, but it was such a blessing to have an older woman who cared for us as she did."

Vonnie Hinkle went home to be with the Lord in 2019, but she left a rich legacy of friendships she had forged like the one she had with Aimee Mestler.

Whitney Harrison's husband, John has been involved with CBMC in the Twin Cities of Minneapolis/St. Paul, Minnesota since 2014. It has provided a number of benefits, she said, including the support and encouragement for being the spiritual leader she has desired for him to be.

"I'm a very strong woman with a successful practice as a certified financial planner, and I'm well-known in the business community, but for me to submit to my husband is very important in our marriage. We both believe God created men to be the head of the household, and knowing John is in line with the Holy Spirit makes it easier for both of us to keep our focus on the Lord," Whitney said.

She expressed her appreciation for the model CBMC has provided for how to integrate one's faith in the business and professional world.

"Before being introduced to CBMC, he had never seen faith being played out in the workplace or other areas of life. He's gained a support system of friends who have taught him that it's okay to pursue a different way of living than what we typically see in the business world. It's a platform he didn't have previously – a place where he can ask questions, an outlet where he can be himself, be vulnerable and grow spiritually, personally and professionally."

The real-life examples her husband has observed and rubbed shoulders with through CBMC have helped him understand what it means to make Jesus Christ the center of every area of life, she observed.

"They have enabled him to become the mentor, guide and support for our family and friends. He's having an impact on people around him in such a different way now – they look up to him and admire what they see of Christ in him. They see how he handles trials and the difference the Lord has made in his life.

"The book of James talks about the wisdom that comes from above, enabling us to be peace-loving, considerate, submissive, sincere, full of mercy and good fruit. John has always been my best friend, but I see those traits in him so much more," Whitney said. "CBMC has helped him to learn how to go to God for wisdom and discernment. I know that he will lead us to all the right places – because his heart is in the right place.

"God has given us different gifts and distinct roles in our family, but John leads our faith daily, and when it comes to our time with the Lord and how we make decisions, it's very obvious that he is the spiritual head."

Whitney said she was involved in an effort to develop a women's counterpart of CBMC in the Twin Cities. "I was actually part of that group. We even had a female Forum. It was good, but I stepped away because John and I wanted to be pouring into the ministry of CBMC together."

For her, CBMC is a ministry where both husband and wife can minister and grow.

Chapter 18

To the Next Generation – and Beyond

"One generation will commend your works to another;
they will tell of your mighty acts." – Psalm 145:4

The true test of a leader is not what happens under his watch, but what continues after he is gone. Does the work continue? Will it grow? The same applies to organizations, including ministries like CBMC. It is especially vital for ministries not to rest on their proverbial laurels and heritage, but to ensure that what they're doing will continue bearing what Jesus, in John 15:16, called "fruit that will last" – for eternity.

Nearing its 90th anniversary observance in 2020, CBMC leaders already were envisioning and prayerfully planning for the years beyond. What steps could be taken to sustain and build on its faithful commitment to evangelism and discipleship? When the time came for a centennial celebration in 2030, what would CBMC be doing to continue its work to advance the kingdom of God in the marketplace?

In 2017, soon after Bill McAvinney became CBMC's President, he with Mark Whitacre and others began praying about God's will for the ministry moving forward. They developed a plan for strategic growth across the United States, with special emphasis on raising up the next generation of young professionals committed to serving Jesus Christ in the marketplace.

"For a time, CBMC was shrinking in size. There were less than 260 cities where we could identify teams of men," McAvinney said. "We were interested in going wherever God was working – small towns, mid-sized cities and large metropolitan cities."

Vision 650 was initiated in October 2017 with the goal of establishing the work of CBMC in 650 cities with 1,200 teams by October 2028. This vision had a number of key elements: starting the ministry in new cities, establishing new teams in existing cities, and expanding the number of Pauls and Timothys meeting together in *Operation Timothy.* "We also wanted to multiply our Young Professionals groups to get more young men involved in CBMC and its mission," he explained.

In the 1980s, CBMC had launched a growth program called Metro 80:80, aimed at planting CBMC groups in the 80 largest cities in the United States during that decade. Although well-intended, it fell far short of its mark, partly because many of the target cities had no one already there poised to lead the way. Vision 650 would take a decidedly different approach.

"We determined our focus in Vision 650 was to locate cities where God is already at work, raising up men who desired to be involved in CBMC or wanted to participate in getting something started where they were," Whitacre said. "We definitely want to make sure God shows up first. Every week at our national Ministry Support Center we receive contacts from people reaching out and wanting to know how they can get involved with what we're doing. Typically, they either ask if there is a CBMC group already in their area, or want help with getting the work started in their city."

Over the first two years of Vision 650, results were very encouraging. By the end of 2018, CBMC was ministering in 301 cities with a total of 481 teams, and by the middle of 2019, those numbers had grown to 324 cities and 526 Connect3, Trusted Advisor Forums and Young Professionals (YP) teams combined.

Looking at CBMC-sponsored events and total participants, the growth was equally impressive. In 2014, for example, there were 175 outreach events with 21,553 attendees. By 2018, those statistics had grown to 429 total events and 48,607 attendees.

Some of CBMC's newer or reestablished cities included Nashville, Tennessee; San Diego, California; Dallas and Austin, Texas; Columbus, Ohio; Glens Falls, New York; Birmingham, Alabama; Tupelo, Mississippi; and Phoenix, Arizona.

Don Hoffert for years has overseen the development of Trusted Advisors/ Forums groups for CBMC, with all training for Peer Advisory Group leaders taking place in Minnesota. He said a microcosm for what God has been doing across the country could be found in his home state of North Dakota.

"Early in 2019 we made presentations in five cities in five days – Grand Forks, Minot, Williston, Dickinson and Bismarck. We received more than 80 names of men in those five cities, and by June each city had set up at least one team. One leader in Bismarck said for 2½ years he had been praying for a group of men in leadership roles to get together to support each other in their faith. He just needed a way to connect them – and CBMC became God's answer to his prayer."

Hoffert explained how the idea of connection resonated strongly with the men. "When we talk about Christian Business Men's Connection, we talk about three things: Up-reach individually to Christ; in-reach to one another in our teams; and outreach to the people God brings into our lives for the Gospel.

"Around the United States we have 600 members of Forums groups, and 220 of them are in North and South Dakota, Minnesota, and western Wisconsin. In Brainerd, Minnesota alone, we have five groups with a total of 50 business leaders, all meeting regularly to strategize on how God can use them in their community."

However, numbers were not and would never be the goal, McAvinney emphasized. "Our goal is planting the seeds of spiritual reproduction in men's souls, so they are compelled to keep doing so for the rest of their lives, whether through CBMC or wherever the Lord leads them. We want to plant thousands and thousands of men equipped, trained and inspired, with confidence they too can impact men of all ages in the marketplace to carry out the Great Commission.

"It's not about a number count – it's about spiritual fruitfulness. We just have to follow the relationships God brings into our lives. Numbers are only affirmation that we're accomplishing something of eternal value and impact."

Underscoring this was "4G Impact," a description for the multi-generational scope of Vision 650. This name was drawn from 2 Timothy 2:2, which encapsulates taking discipleship and spiritual multiplication to a fourth generation. The verse states, "The things which you have heard from me in the presence of many witnesses, these entrust to faithful men who will be able to teach others also."

"We have to be praying for God to enable CBMC to extend its reach to a total of 650 cities and communities, with our ministry of evangelism and disciple-making going to the fourth generation and beyond of spiritual reproducers," McAvinney said.

Whitacre cited himself as an example of 4G Impact played out in real life. In 1998 he encountered CBMC for the first time through Ian Howes, a CBMC member who reached out to help him during a desperate time. Howes discipled him, first using *First Steps* and then *Operation Timothy*, and over the years afterward, Whitacre invested his life into dozens of other men. Together, the spiritual lineage of Howes and Whitacre extends to six generations and is still growing.

Working with Dan Shock, a Desert Storm combat veteran and CBMC Area Director in the Tampa Bay area of Florida, Whitacre spoke at the inaugural Marketplace Ambassador Initiative event in 2015, seeking to launch new teams and revitalize ministry in the area. At the time only a handful of CBMC groups were meeting there, with about 30 men participating on a regular basis.

After the MAI luncheon, where they presented the 10 Attributes of a Marketplace Ambassador, several follow-up meetings were held and new groups started almost immediately. One of those groups was a new initiative called Young Professionals or simply, "YP." By 2019, the number of teams had multiplied, including seven Young Professionals teams, with more than 150 men attending weekly activities throughout the area, and thousands more being impacted by the many in-reach and outreach events being conducted with the goal of reaching and developing men for Jesus Christ.

When a new Young Professionals team is started, the men meet monthly and go through a proven structure through which they learn principles of discipleship and lifestyle evangelism. Christian CEOs and executives visit from the local ministry to share real life "secrets" to their success. The young, emerging leaders also learn to formulate a personal mission statement that helps them, as it did the apostle Paul, to stay the course – to live "on mission."

YP members also spend time helping one another think and pray through their work and life issues through roundtable discussions. The goal is to eventually go through *Operation Timothy* together, with more spiritually mature men leading newer believers through *OT.* Then they are ready to find someone else to take through *Operation Timothy.*

Bo Partin was among the young professionals who benefited from CBMC's presence in the Tampa Bay area. Soon after he had relocated there, he was contacted by Shock through a series of connections. One of Shock's "Pauls" was Norm McClellan, a seasoned CBMC national staff member who had helped him discover his calling to serve in a staff role for CBMC Tampa Bay. McClellan had also influenced Partin's former boss. So, when that man and Shock were introduced by McClellan, he fervently requested that someone reach out to Partin. Shock agreed to do so and pursued Partin with the same spiritual fervor.

Even though he considered himself a Christian, Partin did not attend church and never considered opening a Bible. When Shock invited him to go through *Operation Timothy,* that proved to be a turning point. "I finally agreed to meet with Dan, which became my introduction to CBMC. He never let me out of his grip."

A year and a half after their first meeting, Partin prayed to receive Christ. This continuing relationship, along with new involvement with CBMC, helped him to become established in his faith. Then in 2015, Shock introduced Partin to another CBMC Tampa Bay volunteer leader, Todd Hopkins, the founder and CEO of a commercial cleaning franchise company. Together they became part of the first Young Professionals group in the Tampa Bay area.

For men under 40, YP can serve as a lifeline as they seek to integrate their faith and work, Hopkins said. "These guys are learning about life-on-life together. Many of them have told us they didn't know there were other young Christian businessmen out there.

"The fact is, there are thousands of them out there. They're just not connected. We're seeing young guys popping up everywhere, many of them just out of college, hungry and eager to learn about how to live out their faith."

Partin agreed, speaking about his own team. "This group of guys has been with me every step of the way, through my getting married and starting a family, all while growing a business. Most guys show up looking for some business best practices or how to apply biblical principles to their business. And we offer a great platform for that. But it's the devotion time and roundtable discussions that really get us engaged. This is where authentic sharing and real relationship-building happen."

In years past, CBMC had made efforts to reach out to young business and professional men, but Shock helped to formulate a specific strategy for appealing to men 25-40 years of age through Young Professionals.

"Like business owners and top executives involved with Forums, we consider Young Professionals a Peer Advisory Group, men getting together with their peers sharing common needs and interests, building a relational ministry team," he said.

"The CBMC ministry was becoming very gray, not only in color of hair but also in methodology. We needed new blood and new direction to help the ministry continue its march through time successfully bearing fruit and connecting to the Lord."

Shock said the principles didn't change. The concept of Marketplace Ambassadors resonated with younger business and professional men, as well as the Great Commission mandate calling them to evangelize and become spiritual reproducers. What needed to change was methodology.

"If something is of the Lord, we must be very sensitive to how He wants to do things," he observed. "We've seen things rapidly changing, both from technological and cultural perspectives. I remember the time a young professional I was meeting with let me drive his new Tesla electric car. I was amazed. These guys have electric scooters, and have grown up with smartphones, social media and online digital meetings. A working man's definition of culture is 'how we do things around here.' We need to understand that and respond accordingly."

This did not mean CBMC needed to react impulsively, but to take a prayerful, Spirit-led approach, Shock said. "Being like the men of Issachar described in 1 Chronicles 12:32, who understood the times and knew what they should do."

At the same time, this also did not mean younger men needed to isolate from older men in CBMC. "I was fortunate to be led by the Lord to men who had walked with God for several decades when I got involved with the ministry as a young man. They poured into me and taught me how to spiritually reproduce at the Lord's direction. Younger guys want to learn from older guys, to benefit from their wisdom and experience," he said.

"I was blessed to be directed to Bill Martin, a CBMC lay leader who discipled me with *OT* when I was 24. The only caveat he made for the inordinate amount of time he spent investing in me was that one day he hoped I also would invest in the lives of other men," Shock said. "YP is how I do that today, and 25 years later Jesus is still guiding, blessing and directing CBMC men.

"Bill is still in my life and seeing the subsequent generations who are reproducing for Christ. Norm has gone to be with the Lord in heaven. Bo is discipling others with *OT*. These men, who were deeply touched by God, taught me about significance and legacy vs. worldly success. We need to stay focused on our mission, because the time is short and the stakes are life and death! Praise the Lord for letting us be a part of His eternal work!"

John Scott Harrison could testify to that truth. He had prayed to receive Christ in his pre-teen years, but admitted, "the world got a hold of me for about 10-12 years." At the age of 25, he determined the time had come to make key changes in his life. Less than two months later he learned about CBMC through Alan Smith, a Minneapolis-St. Paul Area Director, and discovered another world he didn't know existed.

"Growing up attending church in Kansas City, I had concluded you could either be a Christian or a wealthy business guy, but not both," Harrison said. "That was my frame of reference, based on what I had observed. Faith and work didn't seem to go hand in hand. But becoming involved in CBMC gave me an understanding of what it meant to be an ambassador for Christ, eliminating the secular-sacred divide I thought existed."

Attending a Connect3 meeting in Minneapolis, he was impressed by the vulnerability of the men he met, their sincere interest in him and willingness to share about their own failures and mistakes, as well as their successes. "Exactly what the business world teaches you not to do – be vulnerable."

Harrison soon found there was much they could teach him, not only about his personal and professional life, but also his spiritual life. "These became guys I wanted to model my life after. My wife, Whitney, said I became a better husband because of it, and my business acumen quadrupled because of relationships I built through CBMC. I found I could go into just about any city in the United States and contact someone who's involved in CBMC. I became sold on it!"

He soon developed a burden for introducing many other men in his generation to what CBMC had to offer for them. "Studies have shown only four percent of my generation are actively going to church. There are many who are unsaved. That means if I meet 100 guys, in all probability only four are going to church or actively engaged in living out their faith on a daily basis. Most people my age aren't going to find Jesus Christ in church."

As a member of CBMC's Young Professionals Advisory Team, Harrison became actively involved in exploring ways to attract more younger men, primarily between the ages of 23 and 40, to the mission of CBMC. With his background in developing business strategies for companies seeking to optimize what they do, he was well-suited for this role.

Harrison said he used John 10:10 as a source for motivation. "In the first half of the verse, we're told the devil comes to steal, kill and destroy. He wants to destroy marriages, families, careers, our lives. But in the second part of the verse, Jesus said He came that we might have life – and have it to our fullest.

"Everybody is after the most fulfilling, joyful life they can have. Experience has already shown me that if we search for fulness in this world, we'll be emptier than ever. There's absolutely more fulness in Christ than in any other way. I often tell people: Don't miss out. Don't miss out on what God has for you."

In addition to his role as Area Director in Tampa Bay, Shock added the responsibility of leading the charge for developing YP groups across the country. Among the first cities he focused on were Raleigh, Ft. Lauderdale, Oklahoma City, Atlanta, and partnered with Alan Smith, a key CBMC leader, in the Twin Cities of Minneapolis and St. Paul.

"I've never seen another initiative like YP," Shock said. "We're having great success in drawing young guys whose cups aren't already full, who don't feel like they've learned it all. And sometimes when executives are asked to sponsor a table at one of our events, they have trouble filling them. I just tell them if they agree to sponsor, our young guys will fill them. I've never had a CEO decline that kind of deal. God's favor is apparent!

"Younger men want to be involved in things where they understand the purpose and it aligns with their values and beliefs. Mainly, they want to connect and get with somebody who truly cares about them."

Derrick Mestler fit that description. As with Harrison, involvement with CBMC helped him to dispense with what he termed a "two-story" perspective of life and work. When he attended the annual Leadership Prayer Breakfast in Fredericksburg in 2013, he indicated on the registration card his desire to know more about CBMC. He had never connected the terms "Christian" and "businessmen" before and wanted to learn how that worked.

About two months later, Mestler met with Bill McAvinney for lunch, marking the start of a strong friendship. It also served as an example of how men in CBMC work together in their shared mission. When McAvinney asked how it happened that Mestler attended the Prayer Breakfast, he answered, "You invited me." "I don't even know you," McAvinney replied in surprise. "You invited the entire Fredericksburg Leadership alumni," Mestler responded, referring to a training program for young local leaders in which he had participated.

Suddenly understanding, McAvinney said, "Well, maybe I invited you, but one of our CBMC leaders, Ron Riblet, covered the meals and costs for everyone who attended as a guest."

As their conversation continued, Mestler explained that even though he had grown up as a Christian, he was still curious about how faith and work could intersect rather than be regarded as totally unrelated aspects of life. McAvinney proceeded to tell him a little about CBMC and its ministry in the marketplace.

"When he showed me CBMC's twofold purpose – 'to present Jesus Christ to business and professional men, and to develop Christian businessmen to carry out the Great Commission' – a light bulb went off in my mind. Finally, I could make sense of it all, how my faith and my work could fit together," Mestler said.

"Until then I had held a two-story view of a secular vs. sacred mentality of life, seeing my personal life and church work as separate from my career. Now I could come to terms with how to live my life for Christ in the 'secular world.' I realized it didn't have to be a struggle to reconcile the two.

"We discussed how being a Christian relates to all aspects of our lives. Then Bill made a statement I'll never forget. He said, 'You've got a target on your back.' This meant he was pursuing me to get involved in the ministry of CBMC. I found it so encouraging to know that this man, whom I barely knew, was taking interest in me."

Mestler was vice president of human relations for a local hospital when they met. Later, when circumstances at work changed, he was faced with a major career decision, including the possibility of moving his family to Florida.

"I had sensed for a while that God was planning some changes in my life," Mestler said. "I didn't fully understand it at the time, but the Lord had His own timetable and was setting things up for my transition."

Instead of accepting a transfer to Florida, he opted to try HR consulting, before accepting an offer to join McAvinney's company in 2016. When

McAvinney was asked to serve as President of CBMC, Mestler agreed to take on greater leadership responsibilities with the firm. This proved to be more than a change in careers. This gave him the opportunity to become more deeply involved with CBMC in Fredericksburg.

He regularly attended two Connect3 teams, including a Young Professionals group, and began meeting with two men in discipling and mentoring relationships. "This matches up with how I'm wired. I see relationships as keys to how life works. I now understand I can share Christ through these relationships. Business is where I spend the major portion of my time, so it opens doors for investing in the lives of guys who don't know Jesus, as well as those who do know Him but – as was the case for me – don't know yet how all the pieces fit together.

"Through CBMC, I've come to understand my calling. It opened up my perspectives, showing me that life in general, everywhere I am, is where I serve the Lord. There aren't any walls anymore, no two-story model. It's just life in all of its aspects."

One question CBMC has faced is how to have a significant impact in the largest U.S. cities, those where they knew of no "man in Macedonia," whom the apostle Paul envisioned in a dream pleading for help. One possible solution to that dilemma was collaborating with the Korean CBMC of North America, which operates independently but shares the same marketplace mission.

In 2019, Whitacre spoke to the 24th Korean CBMC of North America convention in Dallas, with about 300 people in attendance. He found the event inspiring and invigorating. Across the country, including 30 of the largest U.S. cities, about 2,000 men of Korean ethnicity are actively involved in the ministry, he said.

These unique groups have provided a pathway for growing CBMCs directed toward natives of South Korea, people who immigrated to the United States from there early in life, and American-born men of Korean descent. In addition, Whitacre noted, these men in the marketplace – especially younger Korean-Americans born in the United States who often do not even speak Korean – could provide a natural connection with their non-Korean colleagues and peers.

As noted earlier, sheer numbers have not been the focus for CBMC and its leadership. Isaiah 60:22 declares "one shall become a thousand," and through spiritual multiplication, a relatively small but determined, Spirit-filled core of men can accomplish more than they could even imagine.

Many years ago, 18th century theologian and missionary John Wesley wrote:

"If we had three hundred men who feared nothing but God, hated nothing but sin, and were determined to know nothing among men but Jesus Christ and Him crucified, they could set the world on fire."

Addressing attendees at a convention in the early days of CBMC, Dr. Charles E. Fuller, a noted speaker on the "Old Fashioned Revival Hour" radio program, prophetically declared, "Eternity alone will reveal the great number of souls in glory, because faithful Christian laymen are diligent in their businesses, fervent in spirit, and instant in serving the Lord."

Many decades later, this remains true as members of C3 teams, Forums, Young Professionals and other CBMC groups – viewing themselves as marketplace ambassadors – carry on the rich traditions and build on the solid foundation of faithful, visionary Christian businessmen who first gathered in 1930 to respond to the spiritual bankruptcy afflicting their cities and the nation.

McAvinney said he appreciates the legacy of those who have gone before and foresees CBMC continuing to build on that and experience even greater fruitfulness. "The way I see it, CBMC teaches men how to walk forward when others want to hesitate."

McAvinney explained one of his points of emphasis: "To implement a culture of serving with the fervor of a start-up organization, compelled by our mission, and capitalizing on the experience and resources of our 90-year-old ministry. Let us not fall into a season of self-preservation, as some ministries unfortunately have done in the past, but to press on with a sense of purpose and fervency, our course being set on the prize so that nothing can deter us."

He said there was great importance in assessing the present in terms of anticipating what God wants to do in and through CBMC in the future.

"Looking ahead to CBMC's 100th anniversary in 2030, we're praying for an increase of 6,000 men faithfully applying the Scriptures to their lives, 6,000 men praying for the lost using our '10 Most Wanted' card (meaning they are praying for a total of 60,000 other men – or more), 600 more outreach events, 3,000 more disciple-makers, and 600 more teams.

"When I speak, I often say: 'I have one question for myself as well as for you: Is the life I am living worth Jesus dying for?' There's no question that in CBMC, God has given us the training, equipping, encouragement and inspiration we need for truly living lives that were worth Jesus dying for."

Appendix 1: Calling and Mission

Arnold Grunigen, one of CBMC's founders in the 1930s, compiled a list of 12 points defining CBMC's unique calling and mission, which he presented at an early convention:

1. "Christian Business Men's Committee operates that we might tackle men of our size for the Gospel. It trains us, as witnessing Christians – to think – which is hard, before we act – which is so easy.

2. "CBMC is not formed to indulge our appetites, to feed our fancy with strange doctrines, peculiar twistings of scripture truth, or fanciful views of the same. We forget some of the timeworn phrases; we pass over some of the old forms; we re-express its convictions, we restate them to fit the times in which we find ourselves. We are not bound by theological language which has been approved by the seal of approval agencies. We do not have to have a ready-made vocabulary, that has been approved in high places. Thank God!

3. "This is no grouping for dull or unreflecting men who are full of inertia. We welcome change. We are interested in ideas and plans to be used in aggressive evangelism. This operation is not tradition-bound. It enjoys thoughtfully planned innovations. It is a menace to permanence. It is a training, testing and developing agency for aggressive laymen. It is not a mass movement; it is an operation by a specialist group.

4. "It knows that there are great forces in Heaven and earth than man's philosophy cannot fathom; it does not trust human reason, and it has great faith in God's prescription.

5. "It does not smile at flights of eloquent, windy oratory. It dearly loves pungent, meaningful, clipped sentences from warm hearts of believing men. It has eliminated political expediency from its usual high place in organizational efforts.

6. "It matures and instructs, until it cuts down and reduces and affects control of the following very serious ailments in the body of Christ: pride, ambition, avarice, revenge, lust, sedition, hypocrisy, ungoverned zeal, disorderly appetites in its membership. It makes for disciplined men. It reduces the velocity of the storms enumerated above that constantly trouble life.

7. "It is a vehicle that provides reason for performing what we consider our duty and privilege. Membership obviously exposes us to work, sacrifices of comfort; but it causes us to aim for and achieve targets that are otherwise unrealized.

8. "It has taken a living faith that was often trudging down the trail, often reposing on the shelf to good condition, polished it, brightened it, to make it really live in hearts, lives and testimonies. It's made Christianity, salvation and kindred subjects easy to talk about. It multiplied conversations and contacts, it has cut down hesitation and ambiguities in our approach with the Gospel.

9. "It has been a vital aid in 'putting first things first'; spreading the Gospel has top priority with us. This life-giving recipe is not just a social type to be used in times of national or international emergency.

10. "It has strengthened and bulwarked us against the perplexities that newspapers and radios deluge us with, not to mention the conundrum and riddle of atomic energy, new weapons of war, success or failure of international organizations, and the menace of Russian power. It has delivered us from much uncertainty, because we live and work not for this world, and we know what we believe.

11. "It supplies hope for a decent, tranquil, prospering state amid a muddled world scene. It causes us to be able to meet nearly any temporary exigency. Men ignorant of final causes could not meet or answer these so well.

12. "Finally, Christian Business Men's Committee has really helped in saving us from a crass and a vulgar economy in our various placements of life. We budget our time and strength. Cheap substitutes for real life and living have less appeal. We have experienced the 'much mores' of the Word. The world seems dedicated to the short-run. Under God, and with His help, every day finds us laying plans for the long-run. Tried with like passions, tested in a similar manner, this happy, voluntary, unusual aggregation of twice-born men has declared dividends since the company was first organized. Holy Spirit direction is constantly revered, that there may be no letdown until the upper-taker calls."

Appendix 2: What CBMC Is and Is Not

A statement of CBMC policy was published in a 1950 edition of CBMC *Contact*, the membership publication at that time. It clarified the purpose of the organization for both members and non-members:

"The CBMCI is an association of Christian Business Men's Committees of evangelical faith whose purpose and aim are to make Christ known as Savior and Lord. The only reason for our existence is our objective, and that is to reach men for Christ through ways and means that are not ordinary.

"We seek to accomplish our aims and purposes through the following activities and methods:

"*1. Man-to-man aggressive evangelism.*

"*2. Testifying by our life and conduct that Christianity works.*

"*3. Demonstrating that Christianity works in business.*

"*4. Conducting fellowship activities for the purpose of reaching other men for Christ, such as breakfasts, luncheons and banquets.*

"*5. Burnishing and inspiring fellow Christians into a closer fellowship and devotion to Christ.*

"*6. Evangelizing as God gives opportunity through open-air and jail meetings, service men's centers, county farms, rescue missions, etc.*

"While we are cognizant of the role we play in God's overall economy or program, our prayer is that He will keep us (as well as others) from overestimating our importance. We realize also the necessity of being true to the aims and purposes of our organization. For this reason, we reiterate the position of the International and affiliated committees.

"*We are not:* 1) primarily a sponsoring organization; 2) primarily financial underwriters; 3) booking centers for sundry enterprises; 4) an endorsing agency; 5) anti-crusaders. We believe that the only effective approach to better government and improved world conditions is through and by the proclamation of the Gospel."

For more information about CBMC
or to learn how to become involved, write or call:

P.O. Box 8009

Chattanooga, TN 37414

800-566-2262

Or visit our website:

cbmc.com